Bruce Herman is a sports writer, editor, and consultant based in Blacksburg, VA. Editorial consultant to The Topps Company since 1991, he has contributed to *Sports Illustrated* and many other major publications and has been internationally syndicated by Tribune Media. He has written regularly for Athlon Sports since 1996 and is the author of *Hall of Fame Players: Cooperstown* and *St Louis Cardinals: Yesterday & Today*™.

John Franco, a four-time All-Star, played 14 of his 20 seasons for the Mets. His 1,119 games pitched is a National League record, and his 424 career saves is the most by a left-handed pitcher. Franco was honored with the NL Rolaids Relief Man of the Year award in 1988 and 1990.

Factual Verification: **Jake Veyhl**

ACKNOWLEDGMENTS

"Meet the Mets" (pg.14) by Ruth Roberts & Bill Katz
(c) 1969 Goldenrod Music, Inc. (ASCAP)
Used by permission. All rights reserved.
International copyright secured.

Publications International, Ltd. would like to thank **Andy Fogel** for opening his home and sharing with us his extraordinary collection of Mets memorabilia and artifacts.

PICTURE CREDITS:

FRONT AND BACK COVER: AP Images

AP Images: 3, 10 (left), 11 (top right & right center), 15, 19 (bottom), 20 (top), 21 (bottom), 22 (bottom left), 23 (top left & bottom right), 29 (top), 37, 39, 49 (top), 57, 60 (bottom), 62, 67 (bottom), 76 (bottom), 77, 79 (left), 81 (top), 86 (right), 88 (bottom), 89, 91 (bottom), 92 (top right), 94 (bottom), 97, 100, 101, 116 (right), 122 (bottom), 130 (right), 131 (top & bottom right), 137 (bottom), 140 (right); **© Corbis:** 26 (right), 51 (bottom left), 64 (top right), 66 (top left), 78, 85; Bettmann, endsheets, 8 (left), 12 (right), 18 (bottom), 21 (top), 30 (bottom), 42, 44, 48 (left), 49 (bottom), 52 (bottom), 68 (left), 73 (bottom left), 81 (bottom), 87, 95 (left), Tomasso DeRosa, 123; Gary Hershorn/Reuters, 114; Justin Lane/epa, 131 (bottom left); Noah K. Murray/Star Ledger, 129 (top right); Reuters, 103, 109, 125 (top); Ron Sachs/CNP, 136 (top); Ray Stubblebine/Reuters, 102 (bottom), 119 (bottom); Jason Szenes/epa, 141; **Andy Fogel Collection:** contents, 10 (right), 11 (left), 14, 16 (top right), 17 (right), 18 (top), 19 (top), 22 (bottom right), 24 (top left), 25 (right), 26 (left), 28 (top), 29 (bottom), 30 (top), 38 (left), 40 (left), 46 (bottom right), 47 (left & right center), 48 (right), 53 (left), 55, 61 (right), 65, 72 (left center & right center), 76 (top), 80 (top), 82 (right center), 83 (left center & right center), 84 (right), 86 (left), 92 (left center), 98 (left & top right), 99 (center & top right), 102 (top), 106 (top), 107, 112 (left, top right & bottom), 113, 116 (left), 117 (left), 120, 121 (top left & bottom), 122 (top), 126 (left & top right), 127 (top left), 130 (left), 132 (left & center), 133 (top right & bottom right), 137 (top), 138, 139 (top left), 140 (left), 142; **Getty Images:** contents, 6, 12 (left), 45, 53 (right), 63, 70 (top), 71, 90, 94 (top), 96, 104, 105 (top left & top right), 108, 110 (bottom), 115, 119 (top), 124 (top right), 125 (bottom), 128, 129 (top left), 134, 135, 136 (bottom); AFP, 105 (bottom), 110 (top), 111, 117 (right), 118, 124 (left); Diamond Images, 27, 66 (bottom); Focus on Sport, design element background, 32 (bottom), 33, 38 (right), 56, 88 (top), 91 (top); Michael Ochs Archives, 23 (top right); MLB Photos, 7 (top), 28 (bottom), 51 (top), 68 (right), 74 (bottom), 95 (right); *Sports Illustrated*, 9, 35, 50 (left), 59, 69 (right), 70 (bottom), 79 (right); Time & Life Pictures, contents, 13, 22 (top); **Photography Courtesy HA.com:** 17 (bottom left), 23 (left center), 24 (top right & right center), 25 (top left), 40 (top right & bottom right), 46 (left center), 54 (top left & bottom left), 64 (left center), 82 (bottom), 92 (right center), 93 (top left & bottom), 133 (bottom left); **Hunt Auctions:** 8 (right), 16 (top center, left center, center & bottom left), 17 (top left), 25 (top center & bottom left), 32 (top), 34 (top), 40 (center), 41 (right), 46 (bottom left), 47 (top right), 52 (top), 54 (center & top right), 92 (bottom left), 93 (top right & left center), 99 (left), 112 (right center), 121 (top right), 127 (bottom), 129 (bottom), 133 (top left), 143 (top & bottom right); **National Baseball Hall of Fame Library, Cooperstown, N.Y.:** 41 (top left), 50 (right), 69 (left), 75, 80 (bottom), 143 (bottom left); Milo Stewart, 7 (bottom), 40 (bottom), 124 (right center); *New York Daily News:* 20 (bottom), 34 (bottom), 74 (top), 126 (bottom right); **PIL Collection:** contents, 16 (bottom right), 24 (center & bottom left), 41 (bottom left), 46 (top right), 51 (bottom right), 58, 60 (top), 61 (left), 64 (bottom left & bottom right), 66 (top right), 67 (top), 72 (bottom left), 73 (top left, top center, top right & bottom right), 82 (left center), 83 (top left), 84 (left), 98 (bottom right), 106 (bottom left & bottom right), 127 (top right), 132 (right), 139 (top right & bottom); **Transcendental Graphics:** 31; **Wire Image:** contents, 36

Photography: Thomas Kelly – Kelly/Mooney Productions; Peter Rossi/PDR Productions

Front Cover Colorizing: Lisa O'Hara, Wilkinson Studios, Inc.

Being part of Metdom—whether as a player, coach, or fan—isn't always easy. Take it from Casey Stengel, seen here on one of his good days.

Contents

Casey Stengel

1969 Banner

Tom Seaver

Gary Carter

2000 World Series Signed Ball

David Wright

FOREWORD

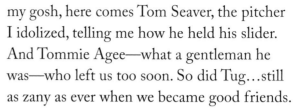

Growing up in the Brooklyn projects, you either rooted for the Mets or the Yankees. Building 5 were the Mets fans; Building 6 were for the Yanks. I lived in Building 5. I became a Met fan from my Dad. He was a big Dodgers fan who used to tell me about Sandy Koufax, Pee Wee Reese, Gil Hodges, and Carl Furillo. After they left New York, he went Mets all the way. I wasn't even two years old when the city received a new team, the New York Mets, but between my Dad and my older brother, Jimmy, the Mets soon became my team, too.

My dad would take us to four or five games a year, and we especially loved Picture Day (when the players would come near the stands and sign autographs), bat day, and banner day. In between, Jimmy and I would collect milk carton coupons; twenty coupons got you a seat in the upper deck. I often imagined playing at Shea Stadium someday.

John Franco

I was nine when the Mets won their first World Series. New York City was very proud. I'd sprint home from school to watch the Series games, glued to the TV. Tom Seaver, Bud Harrelson, Tommie Agee, Cleon Jones, Jerry Grote, Jerry Koosman…I was enamored with them all, but Tug McGraw was my favorite.

Years later, when I met all of them, it was literally a dream come true. It was like, oh my gosh, here comes Tom Seaver, the pitcher I idolized, telling me how he held his slider. And Tommie Agee—what a gentleman he was—who left us too soon. So did Tug…still as zany as ever when we became good friends.

There's something about the Mets that gets in your blood. Whatever it was, I had it even when I pitched for the Reds my first six seasons. When Pete Rose was my manager in Cincinnati, the first thing I asked him was, "Hey, do you remember that fight you had with Buddy Harrelson in the '73 NLCS?" He laughed.

Of course, I had to play *against* my childhood favorites back then. I always tried to beat the Mets, but once the season was over, I still rooted for them—like in the '86 World Series. Sitting on the other side, that was *some* team to compete with. They had that swagger. As soon as they went on the field, they knew they were going to win. A part of me wanted to be a part of that.

After the '89 season, my wish came true. I'd heard rumblings I would be going to the Yankees. I received a phone call in December and the voice on the other end told me I'd been traded to New York. I was in such a daze that I hung up before it ever occurred to me to ask which team in New York! I had to call back.

For 15 years, I lived my dream. We had some good teams and some that struggled, but I loved every minute of it. One day that stands out for me is when the club graciously

honored me with a pre-game ceremony in 1999 for my 400th save. I received a gift from my teammates, a Harley-Davidson, and here comes none other than Tug McGraw riding it out of the bullpen to home plate. A year later, we played the Yankees in the Subway Series, and that was just a great time for the whole city.

In 2001, one of my fellow relievers, Turk Wendell, made the suggestion that I should be the team captain. He took the idea to manager Bobby Valentine and my teammates voted me captain. I was thrilled, since relievers don't usually get to represent the team. I was doing just that, in fact, at a union meeting in Pittsburgh on September 11 when Don Fehr called my room and said a plane had crashed into the Twin Towers. I called home to tell my wife, Rose, and while we were talking, the second plane went into the second tower. Major League Baseball immediately moved us out of our hotel because it was next to a federal building and put us in a more secluded area in the mountains of Pittsburg. When we returned to New York to play again, it was surreal. Finally, the city could take a break from what happened, if only momentarily and enjoy three hours of baseball. We beat the Braves on Mike Piazza's big home run. It was perhaps one of the most emotional moments in my professional career.

I stayed with the Mets until 2004, and was sad to leave, but I felt maybe I had one more year left in me. I retired after pitching for Houston half a season in 2005, it just wasn't the same for me. I settled back home in New York, where owner Fred Wilpon and his son, Jeff (the COO), created a way for me to renew my association with the team. I represent the club in various ways. Some of my duties include marketing, TV, charity events, and trips to spring training to work with the young guys. I visit the ballpark frequently and I was honored to throw out the first pitch ever at Citi Field when my alma mater, St. John's, played there.

The Mets gave me the opportunity to play in front of my friends and family, and become part of their great tradition. Readers of this book have their own opportunity to share in that tradition. From the day my dad said goodbye to his Dodgers, to the original Mets he adopted as his own, to the '69 "miracle," to Tug inspiring the '73 club to a pennant, to that incredible '86 postseason, through my long tenure, all the way up to the final pitch of 2009…it's all in these pages. I've often thought that words can't describe the Mets' colorful history, and how lucky I've been to be a part of it. But the words in this book get pretty close.

— John Franco

This jersey, signed by Franco, commemorates his 400th save, which was recorded on April 14, 1999. Franco would go on to save 24 more games in his career.

CHAPTER ONE

MEET THE METS
1962–1968

THE LOSS OF NATIONAL LEAGUE BASEBALL in New York shook the Big Apple to its core. For three-quarters of a century, NL baseball was more cultural phenomenon than mere pastime. After four seasons without it, the breach was sealed by the creation of the New York Mets. The early teams appalled savvy former Dodger and Giant fans with their ineptitude, but nevertheless they spawned endearment and enduring loyalty.

The '62 Mets lost their opener on the road, then they were feted with a ticker-tape parade up Broadway when they returned to NYC. Here, Mayor Robert Wagner (wearing a hat) stands behind GM George Weiss (left) and manager Casey Stengel during the festivities.

Sports bobblehead dolls first made their appearance in the 1950s, but it was not until 1999 that a Major League Baseball team gave one away at a game—a Willie Mays likeness by the Giants.

Opening Day at the Polo Grounds in 1962 was not exactly a standing-room-only affair, as only 12,447 fans showed up. The Mets' first home game was played on a dank, cold day—on Friday the 13th, no less.

A Betrayal, a Ploy, and a Team of Rivals

In 1958, for the first time since before World War I, Ebbets Field and the Polo Grounds sat empty—empty as the betrayed hearts of millions of New York City baseball fans, empty as the hollow souls of opportunistic owners Walter O'Malley of the Brooklyn Dodgers and Horace Stoneham of the New York Giants, who unceremoniously packed up their franchises and headed for the hitherto untapped markets of the West Coast.

True, the Yankees remained, and they were baseball's crown jewel. But it was the National League game that had captivated the coarse ethnic enclaves of Brooklyn as wholly as it did the button-downs of Manhattan's financial and theater districts. Twenty-two times a year, the Dodgers and Giants would take up arms and bats in opposition, and on those days, the city's other businesses grayed to insignificance. Now, the fans of the two teams were forced into an unholy alliance for survival. Willie Mays saying "hey" to San Francisco? Edwin Donald Snider as the "Duke" of…Chavez Ravine?!? A combined 149 years of tradition was stuffed inside moving vans and transported to sterilized cities that most hardboiled New Yorkers had never even visited, nor cared to. Not even another damn Yankees World Series win was less acceptable.

The city was in shock. "All these people seem to be interested in is the fact the Dodgers have gone to Los Angeles," sighed

They've been called the "worst team ever," but to New Yorkers, a terrible NL team was better than no NL team. The inaugural club was clobbered by five or more runs 37 times.

The parameters of the 1961 expansion draft that was staged to stock the inaugural Mets were rigged so to make competitiveness nearly impossible. Veteran Giants catcher Hobie Landrith, who was the first of the 22 players chosen, was significant only because he was later traded for the legendary Marv Throneberry.

Joan Payson may have been a gazillionaire, but she wasn't above showing her true colors by draping a window in her home with this tacky cloth.

Kenneth Keating while campaigning in Brooklyn for the U.S. Senate at the time. "They have no civic enthusiasm. This is our problem."

The problem-*solvers* included Mayor Robert Wagner, who proffered a new city-financed stadium; Joan Payson, part-owner of the Giants who opposed their relocation; and William Shea, an attorney recruited to do the spade work. Shea set in motion a plan for a third professional league—a ploy that was menacing enough to the status quo that Major League Baseball soon agreed to an expansion plan that would include an NL franchise for Gotham.

The details came together in a New York minute. There are various stories about how the Mets got their name; some cite a fan vote, while others suggest that owner Joan Payson plucked the name from a hat. Still others credit the decision to call the proposed team the "Metropolitans" (which toppled other proposed monikers such as "Skyliners," "Bees," and "Burros") to a vote of media representatives. M. Donald Grant, a former Giants board member, was named chairman. Two former Yankee operatives, George Weiss and Casey Stengel, were named the club's first president and manager, respectively. The team colors would consist of Giant orange and Dodger blue. Until a new park could be completed, the Mets would play in what Stengel called the "Polar Grounds"—the Giants' old haunts.

National League baseball was back. If you could call it baseball.

"First Lady" of the Mets

If there was anything Mrs. Joan Whitney Payson loved more than her art collection, it was baseball. With a chunk of her inherited family fortune, she bought a stake in the Giants. Soon after the team abandoned New York, Mrs. Payson decided to raise the stakes.

On the depth of her pocketbook and the breadth of her passion, the Mets were born. Mrs. Payson (who lobbied to call the team the "Meadowlarks") became the first female principal owner of a major North American sports team. Though consummately hoity-toity in breeding and lifestyle, she was a generous and competitive woman who gave her thoroughbred horses names such as "One Hitter" and "Shutout." She ran the franchise benevolently until her death in 1975, after which her heirs almost ran it into the ground.

Eight games into her team's inaugural season, owner Joan Payson needed a vacation. She was waiting at Idlewild Airport (renamed John F. Kennedy Airport in 1963) for her flight to Paris before the Mets even cracked the win column.

The Mighty Casey

As a player, Casey Stengel suited up for five different teams over 15 seasons. He played in three World Series—each time with a New York club (the Brooklyn Dodgers in 1916 and the New York Giants in 1922 and '23).

To the public in 1962, the Mets' first manager was, if not a buffoon, then at least a cartoon. He was a weathered 72 years of age and possessed both the curse of outsized ears and the gift of gab. Casey Stengel often acted the fool, but he was baseball-brilliant and—in contrast to an image that made for great copy and whirring turnstiles—still as sharp as a Tom Seaver fastball.

A former dental school student, "The Old Perfessor" was a tactician of whom another legendary manager, Sparky Anderson, once said, "He knew every move that was ever invented and some that we haven't even caught on to yet." Still, the Yankees regarded Stengel as an anachronism and fired him in 1960, despite the seven world championships he'd delivered.

"At the end of the season, they're gonna tear this place down," Casey told one of his pitchers at the Polo Grounds. "The way you're pitchin', that right field section will be gone already."

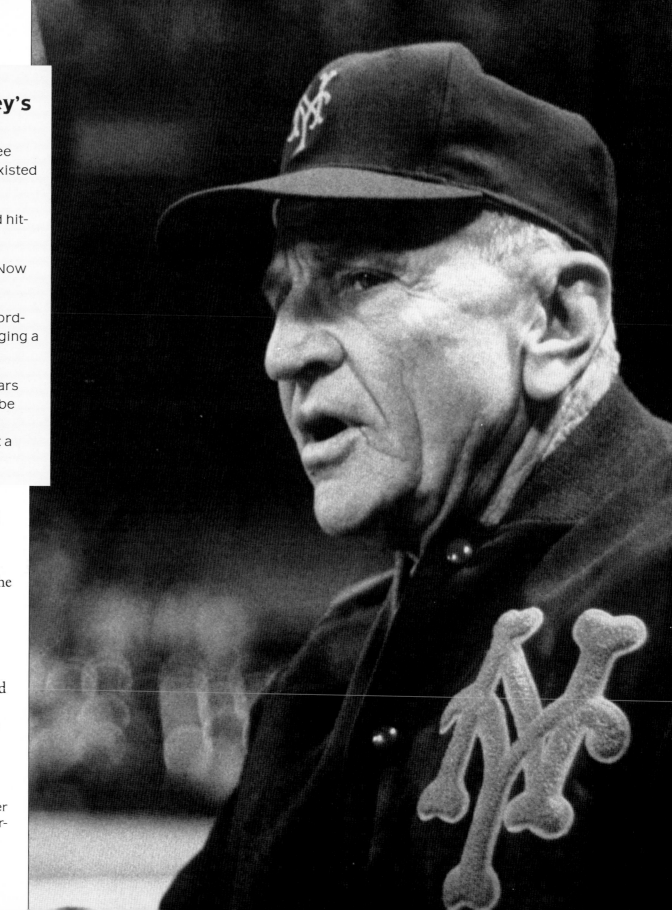

"Stengelese": A Compendium of Casey's Convolution

- "Been in this game 100 years, but I see new ways to lose 'em I never knew existed before."

- "Good pitching will always stop good hitting, and vice-versa."

- "We are a much-improved ball club. Now we lose in extra innings."

- "Everyone line up alphabetically according to your height." (Said while arranging a practice drill.)

- "See that fella over there? He's 20 years old. In 10 years, he's got a chance to be a star. Now that fella over there, he's 20 years old, too. In 10 years he's got a chance to be 30."

A year later, the Mets introduced Stengel as their manager. He promptly told the press that he was thrilled to manage the "Knickerbockers," and went on to become the talent-poor franchise's greatest ambassador, albeit its least successful skipper.

"Nobody would have known about the Mets if it weren't for Casey Stengel," said Don Zimmer, an original Met who managed four big-league teams himself. "Whoever decided to hire him made one smart move."

Stengel managed his last game on July 24, 1965. On that day, his Mets lost on a two-hitter by the Phillies' Jim Bunning, who'd spun a perfect game against them the year before.

From Bad to Worst (Ever)

On the first day, it rained. A suspended sentence. On the second—April 11, 1962, in St. Louis—the Mets attempted to heed their first umpire directive to "Play Ball!" But try as they might, they just couldn't.

Five opposition batters into their existence, the "Amazins" (as Casey Stengel had dubbed them) already had balked runners into scoring position. Twenty-seven innings in, they'd yet to even hold a lead. Nine games in, they remained winless; and after finally beating the Pirates on April 23, they stood eight and a half games out of first place—the closest they'd get all year. New York's new National League team was undeniably pathetic.

This was understandable. Forced to cobble together a roster from a pool of players that was left over after each of the eight established NL teams protected the top 40 players in their organizations, the original Mets were saddled with a compost of has-beens, never-weres, and no-frickin'-chancers.

There was kinetic little Elio Chacon, who took a swing at Willie Mays to ignite the Mets' first brawl; Rod Kanehl, who earned the nickname "Mole" because he was obsessed with riding and memorizing the New York subway system; future U.S. Congressman Wilmer "Vinegar Bend" Mizell; Hobie Landrith, who learned that he'd been traded to the Orioles from his schoolboy son; the unintentionally hilarious Choo Choo Coleman (broadcaster Ralph Kiner: "What's your wife's name and what's she like?" Choo Choo: "Her name is Mrs. Coleman—and she likes me."); an opening-day outfield that holds the unofficial record for children sired (19); and a pair of hurlers named Bob Miller (who also happened to be roommates). The pitching staff had more smarts than stuff: Jay Hook held a master's degree in thermodynamics, Craig Anderson was the first Lehigh grad to pitch in the majors, and Ken MacKenzie described himself as the "lowest-paid alumnus in the entire Yale Class of 1956."

Perhaps the sum damage from that inaugural season shouldn't have been shocking, but it was. The Mets won 40 games and lost 120—still the most defeats in a season since the turn of the 20th century. Bright spots? Outfielder Frank Thomas hit 34 home runs and, well, there were no fatalities.

Few franchises have basked in higher highs or wallowed in lower lows. Despite the plea of this early banner, there is usually little pity for fans of the Mets, whose high profile and deep pockets imply no excuse for under-achievement.

Right: New York infielders made four errors in a 15–1 loss to the Cardinals on July 8, 1962. Although none were by Marv Throneberry, he nevertheless set a still-standing post-World War II record for most errors (17) by a first baseman in fewer than 100 games.

Meet the Mets, meet the Mets,
Step right up and greet the Mets.
Bring your kiddies, bring your wife,
Guaranteed to have the time of your life.
Because the Mets are really sockin' the ball,
Knockin' those home runs over the wall,
East side, west side, everybody's coming down,
To meet the M-E-T-S Mets of New York town.

— Lyrics to Mets' theme song
(by Ruth Roberts and Bill Katz)

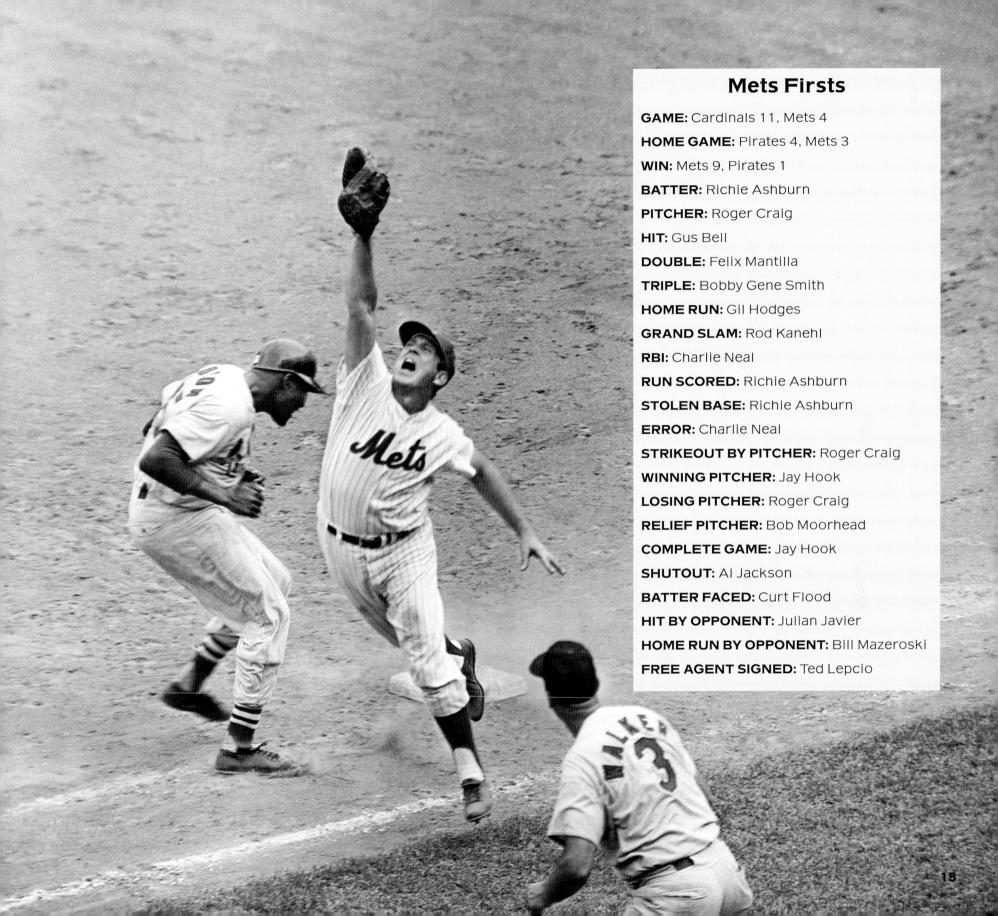

Mets Firsts

GAME: Cardinals 11, Mets 4

HOME GAME: Pirates 4, Mets 3

WIN: Mets 9, Pirates 1

BATTER: Richie Ashburn

PITCHER: Roger Craig

HIT: Gus Bell

DOUBLE: Felix Mantilla

TRIPLE: Bobby Gene Smith

HOME RUN: Gil Hodges

GRAND SLAM: Rod Kanehl

RBI: Charlie Neal

RUN SCORED: Richie Ashburn

STOLEN BASE: Richie Ashburn

ERROR: Charlie Neal

STRIKEOUT BY PITCHER: Roger Craig

WINNING PITCHER: Jay Hook

LOSING PITCHER: Roger Craig

RELIEF PITCHER: Bob Moorhead

COMPLETE GAME: Jay Hook

SHUTOUT: Al Jackson

BATTER FACED: Curt Flood

HIT BY OPPONENT: Julian Javier

HOME RUN BY OPPONENT: Bill Mazeroski

FREE AGENT SIGNED: Ted Lepcio

METS MEMORABILIA

FOR $2.50 IN 1962, A PATRON COULD HAVE PURCHASED A TICKET TO THE METS' VERY FIRST HOME GAME ON APRIL 13. FACE-VALUE PRICES TO THE CITI FIELD INAUGURAL GAME IN 2009 RANGED FROM $19 IN THE OUTFIELD PROMENADE TO $495.

THE COVER OF THE OFFICIAL 1962 SEASON SCHEDULE TRUMPETED THE OPENING OF THE "NEW 1963 HOME." CONSTRUCTION WAS DELAYED, AND THE METS DIDN'T CHRISTEN SHEA UNTIL '64.

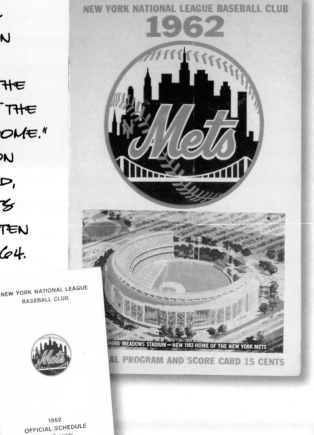

THE POLO GROUNDS CONTAINED 55,000 SEATS, BUT THE METS DIDN'T GET CLOSE TO FILLING THEM. THE OLD BALLYARD WAS STOCKED TO LESS THAN 25 PERCENT OF ITS CAPACITY IN THE CLUB'S TWO SEASONS THERE.

ON THIS PENNANT FROM 1962, THE SILHOUETTE FOR THE NEW TEAM'S LOGO WAS NOT RANDOM. FROM THE LEFT: A BROOKLYN SPIRE, THE WILLIAMSBURG SAVING BANK (BROOKLYN'S TALLEST BUILDING), THE WOOLWORTH BUILDING, THE MIDTOWN SKYLINE, THE EMPIRE STATE BUILDING, AND THE U.N. BUILDING.

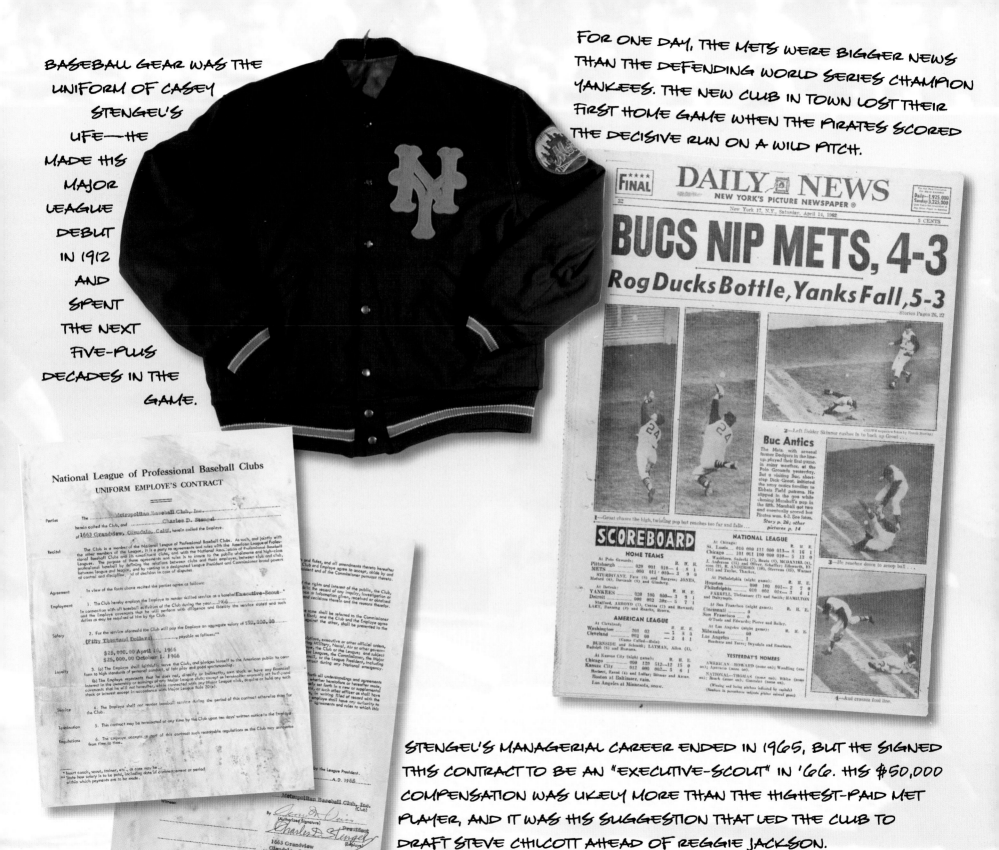

BASEBALL GEAR WAS THE UNIFORM OF CASEY STENGEL'S LIFE—HE MADE HIS MAJOR LEAGUE DEBUT IN 1912 AND SPENT THE NEXT FIVE-PLUS DECADES IN THE GAME.

FOR ONE DAY, THE METS WERE BIGGER NEWS THAN THE DEFENDING WORLD SERIES CHAMPION YANKEES. THE NEW CLUB IN TOWN LOST THEIR FIRST HOME GAME WHEN THE PIRATES SCORED THE DECISIVE RUN ON A WILD PITCH.

STENGEL'S MANAGERIAL CAREER ENDED IN 1965, BUT HE SIGNED THIS CONTRACT TO BE AN "EXECUTIVE-SCOUT" IN '66. HIS $50,000 COMPENSATION WAS LIKELY MORE THAN THE HIGHEST-PAID MET PLAYER, AND IT WAS HIS SUGGESTION THAT LED THE CLUB TO DRAFT STEVE CHILCOTT AHEAD OF REGGIE JACKSON.

17

"Can't Anybody Here Play This Game?"

That's what an exasperated Casey Stengel supposedly asked while holding court in a hotel room on his 73rd birthday in 1962. Answer: Apparently not. Here's some proof from the team's first two zany seasons:

1962

- Jay Hook allowed 17 hits in one inning during the team's first spring training game.

- After Craig Anderson won both games of a doubleheader on May 12, he lost his next 19 decisions and never claimed another big-league W.

- On August 14, Al Jackson worked 15 innings and threw 172 pitches in a losing six-hit effort against the Phillies.

- Don Zimmer endured an 0-for-34 slump; he ended it with a hit off the Phillies' Dallas Green—a future Mets manager.

- Catcher Harry Chiti was acquired from Cleveland in April for a player to be named later. Seven weeks later, he was shipped back to the Indians as that player.

- The Mets hit into a triple play in their last game of the season; the culprit, catcher Joe Pignatano, remains the only known player to do so in the final at-bat of his career.

1963

- During a putrid stretch from mid-June to the end of July, the team dropped 22 straight games on the road.

- In May, the Mets traded an icon—Gil Hodges—for an iconoclast—Jimmy Piersall. A month later, the loopy center fielder ran the bases backward after hitting his 100th career home run, and a month after that he was released.

- Twenty-two-year-old Grover Powell shut out the Phillies in his first major-league start, then became unnerved after taking a line drive to the face off the bat of future Met Donn Clendenon in his next outing. He never pitched in the big leagues again after that season.

- Choo Choo Coleman played 106 games, yet stroked neither a double nor a triple.

- This edition of the Mets was shut out 30 times—still the most in the past 100 years of major-league baseball.

Future Hall of Famers (left to right) Yogi Berra, Warren Spahn, and Casey Stengel were a combined 156 years of age and each just months away from retirement in spring training of 1965.

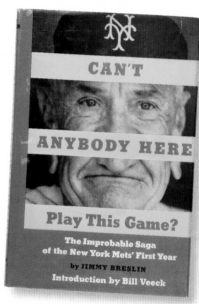

The first important book published about the Mets, Jimmy Breslin's account of the 1962 team was amusing, if not always accurate. He attributed the title quote to Casey Stengel, but later admitted it was fabricated.

Let's Go Mets!

In an eight-million-strong city viral with baseball, there was no shortage of prospective Mets fans in 1960s New York. The team sold nearly a million tickets its first year, an impressive total in those days. But more astonishing than the sheer numbers that poured into the Polo Grounds—a moldering facility that practically begged avoidance—was the unique identity of the faithful. With a chip on one shoulder from the abdication of the Dodgers and Giants and scars on the other from the monopolism of the Yankees, this particular species of fan seemed to revel in its tolerance for pain.

"I've never seen fans like this," marveled pitcher Jay Hook. "They can't afford a big night out, but they'll pay to get into the park….We can be down, 9–0, but they'll be cheering for a rally."

Devotees soon concocted a way for a single voice to rise above the throng—handmade signs began to propagate in the stands as means of self-expression and, often, self-deprecation:

> PRAY!
> WE JUST WANT TO FINISH NINTH!
> TO ERR IS HUMAN, TO FORGIVE
> IS TO BE A METS FAN!

During a 2009 game against the Braves in May, an overzealous fan ran onto Citi Field's newly minted diamond wearing only a thong with a "Mr. Met" doll similar to this one.

At first, curmudgeonly team president George Weiss dispatched security to confiscate every placard it could find. The perpetrators, egged on by an amused media, only showed up with more. In 1963, the club began an annual "Banner Day" contest to find the best one. ("These noisy people with their bed sheets ….Where do they come from?" scoffed Weiss.)

This tradition begat the first Mets "superfan"—Karl Ehrhardt, a German immigrant and disgruntled Dodger fan. For almost two decades, Ehrhardt would arrive at the park armed with dozens of signs from his collection of more than 1,200: They were color-coded, file-tabbed, and ready to be deployed at appropriate moments.

Alas, the popularity of Banner Day gradually dissipated in inverse proportion to the cynicism of the typical baseball fan. In 1996, it was discontinued—a sign of the times.

Cardboard commentary from Karl "The Sign Man" Ehrhardt included, "Look Ma, No Hands," when the Mets made an error. But after the final out of the 1969 World Series, his reverential message was, "There Are No Words."

Falling Stars

Perhaps underestimating the zeal of New York fandom, early Mets executives calculated that the only way to put fannies in seats was to salt rosters with big-name stars. None had much left to offer on the field, but numerous immortals booked the Polo Grounds and Shea Stadium for their farewell tours.

The Mets, by George

George Weiss, the new franchise's de facto COO from 1961 to '66, was a skillful organizer and indefatigable in dedication to his mission, but was also a distant, difficult man to like or work for. He had built a Yankees dynasty through the team's farm system, yet with the Mets, he was preoccupied with signing washed-up ex-stars. Famously, he had to be talked into signing Tom Seaver and out of releasing Jerry Koosman by underling Bing Devine. Weiss left a legacy of losses, but he also built a staff and established an infrastructure that would form the edifice of a champion.

There were smiles all around for (left to right) Mayor Robert Wagner, Bill Shea, Casey Stengel, and George Weiss at the first Mets home game, even though the Pirates won on a wild pitch.

The chronic humiliation of the first season galled no one more than Richie Ashburn, who was the team's MVP and only .300 hitter. By the end of the campaign, it was clear that he could still play a little, but he decided to retire over the winter rather than prolong the agony. Gil Hodges, the outstanding former Brooklyn Dodgers first baseman whose hallowed role in Mets history was yet to be cast, battled kidney stones and a ravaged knee before ending his playing career with the 1963 Amazins.

The Mets purchased arguably the greatest Dodger of them all, Duke Snider, just before the 1963 schedule opened, and he wound up being the team's obligatory All-Star in his final full campaign. Two years later, M. Donald Grant offered $500,000 to the first team that would sell him a future Hall of Famer, but he was rebuffed by the employers of Sandy Koufax, Willie Mays, Hank Aaron, and Billy Williams. He eventually wound up with two anyway—Yogi Berra (for four games) and Warren Spahn, who, after eight straight losses, was waived to the Giants for $1.

With George Weiss (left) as GM and Yogi Berra (right) behind the plate, the Yankees won seven World Series. After Berra was fired as the Bombers' manager in 1964, Weiss hired him as a Mets player-coach.

Marvin Eugene Throneberry

The serendipity of his initials and a few sensationally boneheaded plays made Marv Throneberry the quintessential primordial Met. The first baseman, purchased from Baltimore in May 1962, crafted his legacy a month later. After botching a rundown play against the Cubs, Throneberry apparently atoned for his miscue by hitting a two-run triple, but he was called out for missing first base. Casey Stengel hobbled out to argue, whereupon Mets coach Cookie Lavagetto advised him, "Forget it, Casey. He missed second, too." Throneberry later struck out to end the game with the tying run on first.

"Marvelous Marv" was, from that point on, a folk hero. "Cranberry, strawberry, we love Throneberry!" chanted fans. They especially loved him on August 21, when he pinch-hit a three-run, walk-off homer against the Pirates—and when, after the season's final game, he was awarded

Marv Throneberry was an earnest competitor who hit with some power, but numerous misadventures in 1962 made him paradoxically popular—his thousands-strong fan club donned shirts that bore the letters "VRAM" ("Marv" spelled backward).

Near-Rose Among the Thorns

Somebody here actually *could* play this game. Ron Hunt was purchased from the Milwaukee Braves as a minor-leaguer after the 1962 season and, a year later, finished as runner-up to Pete Rose for the NL Rookie of the Year Award. In 1964, the plucky second baseman became the first Met to start an All-Star Game, doing so before a proud crowd at the newly minted Shea Stadium. Hunt was brokenhearted when dealt to the Dodgers for two-time batting champ Tommy Davis in 1966; he would go on to play several more seasons in the majors and even carved out a painful niche in the baseball record book when he was hit by a pitch 50 times for the 1971 Expos.

Ron Hunt was the Mets' first youthful star. In a 1966 game, his leadoff single was the only thing that deprived Pittsburgh's Woodie Fryman of a perfect game.

a boat for having hit the Howard Clothes advertising signs in the outfield corners more than any other player that year.

Early in 1963, Throneberry was demoted to the minors. Later that year, he got himself locked in the clubhouse after a game; he was released shortly thereafter and retired.

Throneberry reprised his fame two decades later as a star of Miller Lite commercials in which he confessed, "If I do for Lite what I did for baseball, I'm afraid their sales will go down."

Victims of Circumstances

To call any pitcher on those early Mets teams an "ace" requires the broadest definition of poetic license, but chapter and verse on Roger Craig and Al Jackson reveals two pretty fair pitchers. Before joining the inaugural Mets, Craig pitched in three World Series for the Dodgers, while Jackson had been a big winner in the Pirates system. Certainly neither deserved the piteous 55–114 record they compiled for New York between 1962 and '65.

Craig lost 24 times in 1962; no major-league pitcher has lost more games in a season since (though Jack Fisher of the you-know-whos matched it in '65). The next season was even more tragic, as his 5–22 ledger included an NL record-tying 18 consecutive losses, over which he compiled a respectable 4.16 ERA while his teammates gave him all of 1.6 runs per game of support. Finally, on August 9, Jim Hickman's ninth-inning grand slam got the droopy-lidded right-hander off the schneid.

"Little Al" didn't fare any better. Like Craig, the slight southpaw suffered two 20-loss seasons in his time with the Mets. Some days, however, he was unhittable. He spun ten shutouts in four years, two of which were 1–0 gems to defeat the great Bob Gibson (one came on October 2, 1964, a loss that nearly kept the St. Louis Cardinals out of the World Series). Until Tom Seaver showed up, Jackson held every Mets pitching record of consequence.

The belief that this duo was several cuts above their circumstances became more apparent in succeeding decades. A long-time pitching coach, Craig is known as the guru of split-finger fastball instruction (some even credit him with inventing the pitch); he eventually moved on to manage the San Diego Padres and San Francisco Giants with distinction. Jackson, a tremendous communicator, remained in the game until 2000 as a coach and instructor in the Mets and Red Sox organizations.

Al Jackson could be untouchable on any given day—such as on July 21, 1965, when his potential no-hitter against Pittsburgh was broken up by Willie Stargell in the eighth inning. The Mets won, 1–0.

Although hard-luck Roger Craig led the major leagues in losses in both 1962 and '63, there were 164 pitchers whose ERAs were higher during that period.

One of the most obscure pieces of Mets memorabilia is this battery-powered bow tie sold at concession stands during the sixties.

Homes Sweet Homes

Mets attendance jumped 60 percent after they moved into Shea Stadium in 1964. On hand for most games was businessman Herman Ringler, the first customer of its ticket office.

Even after 44 years, Beatlemania remains strong. This ticket stub runs for $200 or more on Internet auction sites.

The Polo Grounds, like the team it hosted, was curiously constructed and well past its prime when it served as the Mets' home in 1962 and '63. It had first hosted baseball games in the 19th century when leased, ironically, by the original New York Metropolitans of the American Association. Its 258-foot right-field wall made a Hall of Famer of the Giants' Mel Ott, but it couldn't help the woebegone Mets, who were anxious for a fresh start in a venue of their very own.

William A. Shea Memorial Stadium, which was named after the lawyer whose string-pulling helped piece together the franchise, was controversial from conception. It took days to decide how many toilets it would house, with the "329" crowd and the "600" faction finally compromising at 526. Most folks were dazzled by the gorgeous interior appointing of the 55,300-seat multipurpose facility in Flushing Meadows; many were less sanguine about its fan-unfriendly dimensions and the garishly aloof orange and blue steel plates slapped onto the façade.

Regardless, the first pitch at Shea—a called strike delivered by "Fat Jack" Fisher—was heaved off its mound on April 17, 1964. But whatever poltergeist had haunted the Mets at the Polo Grounds evidently had wafted its way one borough east; they lost in the ninth inning, 4–3, to the Pirates.

I Wanna Hold Your Band

The Fab Four, who were driven to Shea Stadium in an armored Wells Fargo van, performed 12 songs (beginning with "Twist and Shout") in a half-hour. Ticket prices to the historic concert ranged from $4.50 to $5.75.

Shea staunchly accommodated the Mets for 45 years (and, until the end of the '83 season, the New York Jets football team), but occasionally there were other attractions inside its circular walls. Pope John Paul II, for example, addressed a packed house there in 1979. But the facility never rocked harder or louder than on August 15, 1965, when The Beatles chose Shea as the venue from which they would launch their first full North American tour. Their 12-song set is regarded as one of the most significant pop-culture events of the 20th century. Things came full circle in 2008 when the "Last Play at Shea" farewell concert closed with Paul McCartney's emotional rendition of "Let It Be."

Situated just north of Central Park, the Polo Grounds was demolished after the Mets moved into Shea Stadium—with a wrecking ball painted to look like a baseball.

METS MEMORABILIA

THE 1964 ALL-STAR GAME AT SHEA GAVE THE CLUB A CHANCE TO SHOW OFF ITS NEW HOME. IT WAS ONE OF THE MOST DRAMATIC MIDSUMMER CLASSICS EVER, AS WILLIE MAYS WALKED TO START A FOUR-RUN NATIONAL LEAGUE RALLY CLIMAXED BY JOHNNY CALLISON'S WALK-OFF HOMER.

"MR. MET" MADE HIS FIRST APPEARANCE AS THE METS' MASCOT IN 1963, GRACING THEIR GAME PROGRAMS. A YEAR LATER, HE IS BELIEVED TO HAVE BEEN THE FIRST MLB MASCOT TRANSLATED FROM ARTIST'S RENDERING TO HUMAN CHARACTER FORM.

THIS SONGBOOK WAS CREATED BY JANE JARVIS, SHEA'S ORGANIST FROM 1964 TO '79, WHO LATER BECAME A RENOWNED JAZZ PIANIST. THE PIECE CAME FROM THE ESTATE OF TRAINER GUS MAUCH WHO, AFTER 19 YEARS WITH THE YANKEES, FOLLOWED CASEY STENGEL ACROSS TOWN IN '62.

THIS PIECE OF CLOTH ART, SENT TO HIM BY A YOUNG FAN IN 1963, WAS A GIFT CASEY STENGEL KEPT TO THE DAY HE PASSED AWAY. ANOTHER SECTION OF IT, TITLED "MEET THE METS" (NOT PICTURED), LISTS THE NAMES OF HIS PLAYERS FROM THAT SEASON.

"OLDTIMERS WEEKENDS AND AIRPLANE LANDINGS ARE ALIKE," CASEY STENGEL ONCE SAID. "IF YOU CAN WALK AWAY FROM THEM, THEY'RE SUCCESSFUL." THE 1965 EXHIBITION FEATURED FORMER MEMBERS OF THE NEW YORK GIANTS (SUCH AS HALL OF FAMER MONTE IRVIN, WHO RECEIVED THIS CUP).

THIS 6 1/2-INCH LADY MET SOUVENIR, WHOSE HEAD CAN TURN AND BE POSED, DATES BACK TO THE 1960S. HARDER TO FIND THAN HER "HUSBAND," SHE IS VALUED AT SEVERAL HUNDRED DOLLARS.

THE BIG APPLE'S NEW NATIONAL LEAGUE TEAM WAS OFFICIALLY DUBBED THE METROPOLITAN BASEBALL CLUB OF NEW YORK—OR "METS" FOR SHORT. THE NAME HARKENED TO A TEAM THAT PLAYED IN THE CITY FROM 1880 TO 1887, AND WHO WON THE 1884 AMERICAN ASSOCIATION PENNANT.

Lose One, Win One

The Mets' booby prize for finishing with the worst record in baseball in 1965 was the first pick in the 1966 amateur draft. One of their scouts, Dee Fondy, was ga-ga over a flashy, powerful outfielder from Arizona State whom some of his peers were comparing to Willie Mays. A retired Casey Stengel, however, had seen a high school catcher in California and came away smitten. "I think the kid was about 16-for-16 when Casey was there," recalled Nelson Burbrink, another club bird-dog. "It was Casey's opinion that we take him." And so, in one of the most inauspicious decisions in their history, the Mets deferred to their patriarch and drafted Steve Chilcott, leaving Reggie Jackson to be selected by the Kansas City Athletics.

Fourteen months later, Jax was commencing his colorful Hall of Fame career in K.C. while Chilcott was nursing a shoulder injury in A-ball that (along with other maladies) eroded his skills so badly that he became the first No. 1 overall draft choice to leave the game without playing a day in the bigs.

They didn't know it yet, but the Mets had actually counteracted this epic miscalculation with a little prescience and a bold stroke of dumb luck just a few months earlier. The rights to pitcher Tom Seaver of USC were up for grabs to any club who wanted to match the voided $50,000 contract offered to him by the Atlanta Braves. Three teams were willing to risk the investment. Slips of paper with the names "Indians," "Phillies," and "Mets" were dropped into a hat, and when the latter was drawn, the course of the franchise was forever altered. Something finally went right.

THROWING OBJECTS OF ANY KIND WILL RESULT IN IMMEDIATE EJECTION FROM THE POLO GROUNDS.

PLEASE CO-OPERATE.

THANK YOU,

NEW YORK METS

The Polo Grounds broke ground in 1890, the same year Casey Stengel was born. This tattered sign hung within its tattered confines when the Mets became its final tenants in 1962.

After the 1966 draft, GM Bing Devine polled other clubs to ask whom they would have taken first. Ten said Reggie Jackson; nine agreed with the Mets' choice of Steve Chilcott.

Signs of Progress

The New York Mets' first five seasons were such tragicomedy that it was hard to imagine any imminent scenario that would prod them along a path to respectability. Health issues forced Stengel to retire in July 1965, and Wes Westrum managed the team to 66 wins (13 more than ever before) and out of the cellar—by only one position, mind you—for the first time in '66. After the season, first-year GM Bing Devine, who had recently assembled a championship team in St. Louis, promptly put the roster in a blender and set it to "frappe."

Half of the opening-day 1967 ball club was new, and the shuffle didn't stop there. Fifty-one different players wore Mets uniforms that year; the new faces included such heroes-to-be as third baseman Ed Charles, pitcher Don Cardwell, shortstop Bud Harrelson, second baseman Ken Boswell, and the brightest jewels of all—pitchers Tom Seaver and Jerry Koosman. However, the end product looked dispiritingly familiar: a 61–101 cellar-dweller.

Something was missing. So "Trader Bing" pulled off his craftiest gambit of all—an unconventional trade for a manager. The Mets acquired esteemed field general Gil Hodges from the Washington Senators for pitcher Bill Denehy and a hundred grand. A week later, Devine abruptly resigned to return to the Cardinals. His successor, Johnny Murphy, quickly bartered with the White Sox for outfielder Tommie Agee and infielder Al Weis.

Amidst all this frenetic personnel jockeying, the Mets' minor-league system, under the direction of Whitey Herzog, was quietly maturing. It had already supplied the 1967 NL Rookie of the Year in Seaver; Koosman would finish second in the NL Rookie of the Year balloting in '68; and fellow moundsmen Nolan Ryan, Gary Gentry, Jim McAndrew, and Tug McGraw were in varying stages of development. Outfielders Cleon Jones and Ron Swoboda were in The Show by this time, but their best baseball was clearly ahead. The same could be said for the Mets.

There was no shame in finishing second in the 1968 NL Rookie of the Year voting. Nineteen-game winner Jerry Koosman was barely edged out of the award by future Hall of Famer Johnny Bench.

Master Ed

The bell curve that was the career of Ed Kranepool is one of the most fascinating in Mets annals. The $85,000 he received as the club's first bonus baby was serious greenage in 1962, and that he was a teenage prodigy from the Bronx—with all the 'tude that goes with that—only added to his allure. The front office couldn't resist slipping the cocky first baseman into a few games before his 18th birthday, and he showed that he belonged by doubling in his first start. By 22, he was a four-year starter and a darling of Metdom.

Lou Gehrig he was not, but in 1964, "Krane" gave the Mets their own version of the "Iron Horse." On May 30, he played every inning of a doubleheader for the Triple-A team in Buffalo, then did the same thing for the big club against the Giants the next day—the footnote being that game two of the second day's doubleheader lasted 23 innings. His 50 innings of action in approximately 34 hours was considered unprecedented.

By the end of the 1960s, though, the honeymoon was over. Kranepool had never hit more than 16 home runs nor batted higher than .269, and he was losing his grip on playing time. Worse, fans had decided that all the hype (and all the money he made) had corroded his motivation.

Another chapter was to be written, however. Between 1974 and '77, he swatted .299, and again the chants of "Ed-die! Ed-die!" cascaded from the stands at Shea. Kranepool became arguably baseball's best bench bat of the era, producing 75 pinch-hits in the 1970s (including a phenomenal 17-for-35 performance in '74).

It was not always a smooth ride for the last of the original Mets, but it was a long one. His seasons served (18), games played (1,853), and total hits (1,418) remain team records by wide margins.

Ed Kranepool was a symbol of fans' hopes for the future. After breaking Hall of Famer Hank Greenberg's home run record at a Bronx high school, he played 361 games for the Mets before his 21st birthday.

This 7-inch-long souvenir megaphone from the 1960s declared the Mets to be "not fancy," but "good." That was certainly true in '69, when the overachievers won it all despite finishing ninth among the 12 NL teams in scoring.

From Tragedy... Togetherness

It was the year Dr. Martin Luther King Jr. and New York Senator Robert Kennedy were assassinated. The U.S. death toll in Vietnam rose past 20,000. Student uprisings slammed colleges shut. Riots turned the Democratic National Convention in Chicago to bedlam. The America of 1968 was pandemonium. Yet in spite of all this, the New York Mets found their equilibrium.

A few days after Kennedy was murdered, the Mets voted unanimously not to play their game in San Francisco on June 8, the day of his funeral. "We're from New York," explained player rep Ed Kranepool. "It's a matter of respect for us not to play." The decision infuriated Giants owner Horace Stoneham (who stood to lose megabucks from the cancellation of his "Bat Day"), but the Mets—from Joan Payson to the clubhouse boy—stood firm.

Even the topic of race, as explosive as it was in the country at the time, was a non-issue for the Mets. Team RBI leader Ron Swoboda shrugged when he got hate mail for inviting the four blacks on the Mets' roster to his home for dinner. And there was no more popular man in the clubhouse than African American third baseman Ed Charles, who topped the squad in homers. This concept of a "unified team" was new for the Mets, and it was amazingly

It wasn't long after "Mr. Met" became the team's mascot that "Lady Met" began popping up—not in person, but in print and on souvenirs. Though her name lent no implication of betrothal, she appeared, at times, with a trio of "little Mets." Years later, the entire family was satirized in an ESPN *SportsCenter* commercial.

galvanizing. Sitting at 21–27 at the time of Kennedy's death, they won 12 of their next 20 games.

Although the 1968 team's 73–89 record seemed innocuous, it was by far the club's best yet. The pitching, especially, was the talk of baseball. Anchored by young All-Stars Tom Seaver and Jerry Koosman, the staff ERA was 2.72—an extraordinary turnaround from the 4.23 mark of the club's first six seasons. The most monumental reversal of all was just months away.

On May 20, 1968, Ed Charles—at 35, a full decade older than any other lineup regular on a simmering powderkeg of a team—provided the only two runs of a game against the Pirates with solo homers, including this walk-off blast.

CHAPTER TWO

A MIRACLE?
"YA GOTTA BELIEVE"
1969–1973

BY THE LATE 1960s, the line between laughing *with* the Mets and laughing *at* them was beginning to blur. Seven seasons into their existence, the team had won barely one-third of their games, but in 1969, their no-nonsense manager and cheeky young pitching staff steered the team into arguably the most improbable turnaround in base-ball history. Four years later, the Mets had a chance to win it all again—if only they would believe.

Gil Hodges' auto-graph alone is one of the most sought after of the past half-century by collectors. A vintage ball in good condition signed by him and the rest of the 1969 Miracle Mets can fetch thousands of dollars at auction.

For Donn Clendenon, a champagne shower "hurt so good" after his three-run homer in the first inning off Steve Carlton sent the Mets on their way to a division-clinching win over the Cardinals on September 24, 1969. Gary Gentry didn't need much help in his four-hit shutout.

There was no attempt to restrain the thousands of exuberant fans who rushed onto the Shea Stadium field after the final out of the 1969 World Series. The grounds crew had just three days to replace 6,500 square feet of grass for an upcoming Jets football game.

Miracle in the Metropolis

Reporters at spring training choked back grins when manager Gil Hodges told them he thought his boys could win 85 games in 1969. Hodges had spent the winter recuperating from a minor heart attack while GM Johnny Murphy spent his rebuffing trade offers for his brilliant kid pitchers. No other young set of arms in the game could match the Mets' quintet of under-27s: Tom Seaver, Jerry Koosman, Nolan Ryan, rookie Gary Gentry, and reliever Tug McGraw. Whether these hurlers could surmount the club's crunchless batting order—not to mention the crush of history—was a different proposition altogether. Eighty-five wins? It would take a miracle.

A quarter-way into the schedule, there was still no hint of divine intervention, as the Mets stood at 18–23. Then there was a crack in the clouds: an 11-game winning streak, which barely made a dent in the NL East standings, but did make a statement—to the players themselves, if not the pundits.

There did, however, still seem to be a force field around home plate. On June 15, Murphy made a move that was designed to address the offensive impotence, wresting big first baseman Donn Clendenon away from the Expos. He proved to be the hammer that was missing from the middle of the lineup, and by the time the division-leading Cubs came to town

in July, the Mets had drawn to within five and a half games. At an apoplectic Shea, the hosts pulled out two unforgettable victories—one on Ed Kranepool's walk-off hit and the other after Seaver retired the first 25 batters. They won two of three at Wrigley Field the following week, lifted by the only two home runs birdish utility infielder Al Weis would muster the entire regular season. After an 11–14 spiral that allowed the Cubs to extend their advantage to ten games by mid-August, New York won 12 of 13 while Chicago bowed in 9 of 14 to taper the margin to two and a half.

On September 8, the Cubs returned to New York for a two-game test of manhood that was spiced by brushbacks and beanballs. As the visitors batted in the first inning of the opener, a black cat materialized on

The pose by Mr. Met on this pennant says it all for Mets fans—after the miracle of 1969, they, too, could stand proud of their team.

Opportunistic defense was a trademark of the '69 Mets. Here, Donn Clendenon (#22), Al Weis (center), and Bud Harrelson (#3) execute a perfect rundown to retire Paul Blair in the World Series.

In four games in the 1969 fall classic, Donn Clendenon hit three home runs—as many as all the Orioles combined.

the field, prowled up to Chicago stars Ron Santo and Billy Williams, pierced both with a malevolent stare, then hissed at manager Leo Durocher before vanishing. The spell was cast, and the Mets triumphed twice, sending their once-brazen nemeses into a panic from which they would not recover. A 12th-inning walk-off RBI single by second baseman Ken Boswell against Montreal the next day slid the Mets into first place. They extended their advantage with a white-hot month that included a doubleheader sweep in which the sole run in each game was knocked in by a pitcher, and a gritty win against the Cardinals—whose pitcher, Steve Carlton, tallied a then-record-setting 19 strikeouts—that was made possible by a pair of two-run Ron

Swoboda homers. It was indeed miraculous: With a 38–11 finish, the team had won 100 games—and the hearts of a captivated baseball universe.

Somewhere, someone asked Casey Stengel what he thought of these newfangled Amazins. "This club plays better baseball now," he replied. "Some of them look fairly alert."

The first-ever National League Championship Series pitted the Mets against Henry Aaron's Atlanta Braves. Both New York's sweep and the manner in which it was accomplished were characteristically confounding—the "all-pitch/no-hit" Gothamites overcame an 8.49 ERA from Seaver and Koosman by scoring 27 runs in the three contests.

The AL-champion Baltimore Orioles, formidable winners of 109 games, seemed more bemused than anything else to be meeting such upstarts in the 1969 World Series. "Bring on Rod Stupid," spat Frank Robinson, the Os' biggest star; the slur was an allusion to substitute outfielder Rod Gaspar, the most anonymous of the no-name Mets. "No idea," Robinson shrugged when asked if he knew who the opposition's starting third baseman was.

The Mets earned no deference after dropping the opener in Baltimore 4–1, but six innings of no-hit ball by Koosman put Game 2 up for grabs. It was 1–1 in the ninth when Ed Charles (the Mets' third baseman, Robinson may have noticed) rapped a single to left to start a two-out rally that was capped by an RBI single by Al Weis. The Mets held on to win 2–1.

Game 3 was distinctly Metsian—a 5–0 shutout by Gentry and Ryan was preserved by two acrobatic catches in center field by Tommie Agee. It was more of the same the next day, as Seaver was brilliant. Yet it took right fielder Swoboda's iconic diving catch in the ninth to prevent Baltimore from walking away with the victory. The outcome was unresolved until the tenth inning, when catcher J. C. Martin bunted and was struck by the throw to first base, allowing none other than "Rod Stupid" to score the winning run. Orioles protestations that Martin was inside the baseline were no match for karma.

Game 5 was a madcap microcosm of the Mets' season. After falling behind 3–0, New York rallied in the sixth. Umpire Lou DiMuro called a ball on Cleon Jones, but after Hodges pointed out a scuff of shoe polish on the orb (imprinted there, as reported by Peter Golenbock, on the manager's order by Koosman), Jones was ushered to first as a hit batsman. Moments later, Clendenon cleared the left-field wall. The absurdly unlikely Weis (who hit a total of eight home runs duing his ten-year career) did the same in the seventh to tie the tilt, and the Mets set the final at 5–3 with a Swoboda RBI double and an unearned run in the eighth. The Mets ... *the Mets!* ... were World Series champions, and somehow a tumultuous world seemed a little better for it.

"I know there were people who changed their lives because of the Miracle Mets. People felt better. It was a good thing," surmised Charles.

"Miracle, my eye," scoffed Tom Seaver.

The "still" part may have been premature, as this was the Mets' first World Series title, a feat that wouldn't be duplicated until 1986.

Right: Jerry Koosman spotted the Orioles three early runs in Game 5 of the '69 Series. He then allowed only two base runners in the final six innings before jumping into Jerry Grote's arms to celebrate the last out of the series.

Below: Rod Gaspar, pinch-running for Jerry Grote (who had doubled), scored the winning run in the bottom of the tenth inning of Game 4 when pitcher Pete Richert's throw to first base caromed off of J. C. Martin, who had laid down a sac bunt.

The Terrific One

In high school, the kid was a .500 pitcher who lugged crates of raisins at a packing company in his spare time. At 5′10″ and (on a dry day in Fresno) 165 pounds, there were no college scholarship offers, so he fulfilled his military commitment before paying his own way to Fresno State, where he might catch the eye of a bigger program—or perhaps study to be a dentist.

The rapidity at which life then unfolded for George Thomas Seaver was dizzying. He earned a ride to USC, priced himself out of a Dodgers offer, saw his contract with the Braves voided by a technicality, and reluctantly signed with the Mets in 1966. Eighteen months hence, the smart and stylish right-hander laid the first brick on his road to Cooperstown by picking up the National League Rookie of the Year. The fledgling New York franchise had its first homegrown star, and to this day, no Met has outshone him in decorum or distinction.

"Seaver had Hall of Fame written on him when he walked into camp and pitched his first game in '67," Ron Swoboda reflected. "He was a finished product...I don't ever recall the sense of him being a rookie." Future Hall of Famer Lou Brock didn't even think

Left: With his classic "drop-and-drive" pitching style, Tom Seaver notched 198 victories in a Mets uniform. Here, he drops an eight-strikeout performance on the Pirates in his MLB debut.

Seaver was not only terrific enough to win three Cy Young Awards in New York, but also to finish second twice—once with the Mets and once with the Reds.

the seraph-face right-hander was a ballplayer—the Cardinals star mistook him for a clubhouse boy at the All-Star Game and requested that he fetch him a beer.

In both 1967 and '68, Seaver contributed 16 wins to Mets teams that were scarcely capable of supporting his brilliance. More importantly, he contributed an attitude never before encountered in the club's locker room. "There was an aura of defeatism," he recalled. "I could not accept that. That lovable loser stuff was not funny to me." He backed this up by going 25–7 with a 2.21 ERA for the 1969 world champions and, over the next eight seasons, winning three Cy Young Awards, a like number of ERA crowns, and five strikeout titles.

Although Seaver and controversy typically avoided each other like Nixon and tie-dye, it did besiege him twice. First, the ex-Marine reservist took a stand against the Vietnam War, which, in 1969 America, automatically split allegiances straight down the middle. Eight years later, he was tabloid fodder for months amidst a feud with chairman M. Donald Grant that climaxed with the beloved pitcher being traded to Cincinnati.

Seaver returned to New York in his career's twilight for the 1983 season. He pitched for three other teams, but when he was inducted into the Hall of Fame in 1992 with the highest vote percentage ever, "Tom Terrific" was wearing the cap of the franchise that he—more than any other man—put on the baseball map.

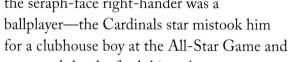

Tom Seaver literally wrote the book on pitching—during his career and in this volume, published shortly after he left New York for the second time. Like Ted Williams' *The Science of Hitting*, it has endured as a how-to classic.

Oh Yeah, Those Other Guys

In a first-rate rotation headlined by Tom Seaver, Jerry Koosman was a second-class citizen and Gary Gentry the third wheel . . . but, man, could they pitch. Kooz was discovered on a U.S. Army team; the son of a Shea Stadium usher had alerted the Mets to his talent. He fired seven shutouts in 1968 and six more in '69 (his first two seasons) and went 4–0 with a 2.29 ERA in his final five postseason starts with New York. The rookie Gentry won 13 times in the regular season plus once more in the World Series for the Miracle Mets. And though the other two 1969 starters lugged losing ledgers, both Don Cardwell (1.82 ERA after July 31) and Jim McAndrew (two August shutouts) were brilliant down the stretch.

Perhaps it's fitting that Jerry Koosman—who outshone the much harder-throwing Tom Seaver in the '69 Series—utilized his engineering degree after retiring to patent a self-cleaning "soft-serve" ice cream machine.

The Day Tom Wasn't Perfect

One would be hard-pressed to find a Cub fan who remembers Jimmy Qualls, even though he played for the northsiders. Every Mets fan on the planet, however, knows exactly who he is.

Shea Stadium was crammed and clamorous on July 9, 1969, for the second game of a series with the Cubbies that could further constrict a dramatically developing pennant race. There was no better choice to take the ball than Tom Seaver, whose career ERA against them coming in was a tidy 1.84. The ace proved that he was the right man for the job, dealing out after out. As New York built a 4–0 lead, tension heightened to a crushing crescendo. Heading into the ninth, Seaver had retired every batter (11 via strikeout)—just

Seaver struck out future Hall of Famer Ernie Banks, but it was unknown Jimmy Qualls who ruined his perfect game three batters later. "I had never faced Qualls before," said Seaver. "I wasn't sure just how to pitch him."

No-Nos, Seven Thousand Times No

The Mets have played 7,644 games without throwing a no-hitter—currently the longest streak in baseball. (Seaver did throw a no-no, but he did it as a member of the Reds.) That said, Tom was more than terrific in these performances:

- **April 22, 1970:** Seaver strikes out the last ten Padres he faces —a record—while tying another with 19 Ks overall.
- **July 4, 1972:** Once again, he sees a no-no go by the boards on a one-out, ninth-inning single, this time by San Diego's Leron Lee.
- **September 24, 1975:** No Cub musters a hit against him until Joe Wallis singles with two outs in the ninth inning of a scoreless game.

a 1-2-3 inning away from the eighth perfect game in modern history.

The air was sucked out of the stadium as Chicago catcher Randy Hundley flouted baseball's unwritten code in that situation by bunting. Seaver, however, fielded the roller and fired it to first base like the potential hand grenade it was. Next up was an unknown 22-year-old outfielder playing in his 18th major-league game. Seaver tried to nick the outside corner with his first pitch of the at-bat but left a fastball over the plate, where Jimmy Qualls whacked it cleanly into center for a single. Two quick outs ended the game, but the bittersweet sting of the Mets' closest-ever brush with pitching perfection remains.

METS MEMORABILIA

THIS PENNANT IS SIGNIFICANT BECAUSE IT REPRESENTS THE FIRST NATIONAL LEAGUE EAST CHAMPIONSHIP IN BASEBALL HISTORY, AS DIVISIONAL PLAY BEGAN THAT SEASON. EVEN IN THE OLD FORMAT, THE '69 METS WOULD HAVE BEEN WORLD SERIES-BOUND WITH A LEAGUE-BEST 100-62 RECORD.

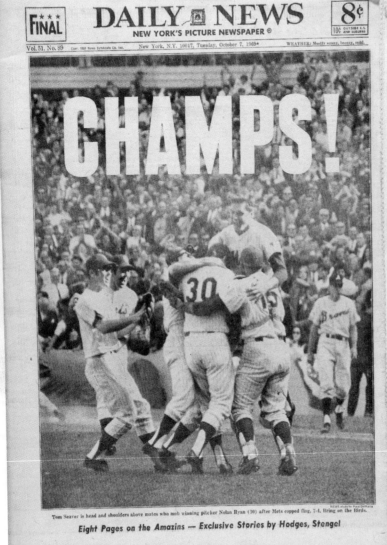

ONE WORD CAPTURED THE CITY'S EUPHORIA WHEN THE METS WERE CROWNED NL CHAMPIONS IN 1969. STARS INCLUDED TOMMIE AGEE AND KEN BOSWELL (TWO HOMERS APIECE), ART SHAMSKY (.538 AVG), AND CLEON JONES (.429 AVG.).

THIS IS A CHARM ISSUED TO CELEBRATE PERHAPS THE MOST CHARMED TEAM OF ALL—THE 1969 "MIRACLE METS."

MEMBERS OF THE MEDIA HAVE BEEN PRESENTED A CUSTOM WORLD SERIES PRESS PIN (ONE FOR EACH TEAM) FOR NEARLY A CENTURY. THIS ONE, MANUFACTURED FOR THE METS BY BALFOUR IN 1973, IS WORTH BETWEEN $175 AND $200.

THIS WORLD SERIES RING WAS PRESENTED TO WARREN GILES, PRESIDENT OF THE NATIONAL LEAGUE FROM 1951 TO 1969.

THE UNIFORM NUMBERS ON THESE CARICATURES REPRESENTED THE BEST OF TIMES AND THE WORST OF TIMES. THE METS TRULY HAD COME OF AGE.

GIL HODGES WORE #14 WHEN HE PLAYED FOR THE METS IN 1962 AND '63, AND HE GOT THE NUMBER BACK WHEN HE TOOK THE MANAGERIAL REINS IN '68. IN BETWEEN, IT WAS IN GOOD HANDS, DONNED BY RON SWOBODA AND KEN BOYER. HODGES'S DIGITS WERE RETIRED IN '73.

BROOKLYN-BASED RHEINGOLD BEER ("IT'S REFRESHING, NOT SWEET. IT'S THE EXTRA DRY TREAT."), TYPICALLY THE CHOICE OF NEW YORK'S WORKING CLASS, SPONSORED METS BROADCASTS INTO THE 1970S. A NEW COMPANY RELAUNCHED THE BREW AT SHEA IN 1998, WITH PROMOTIONAL ASSISTANCE FROM TOMMIE AGEE AND ED KRANEPOOL.

Bridge over Troubled Waters

The fairy tale that was the miracle 1969 season seemed to unfold in a universe that was parallel to the one in which tumultuous political and social events were taking place all over the world. The Mets became "America's team," and following the team's evolution from consummate underdog to implausible champion was a tonic for ordinary Americans who knew little about baseball but craved respite from Vietnam War body counts, race riots, and all manner of cultural revolution.

Only the classic championship teams are tagged with enduring nicknames—the "Bronx Bombers," the "Gashouse Gang," the "Big Red Machine," and these "Miracle Mets."

DATE	FRONT PAGE	SPORTS PAGE
April 9	Students seize the Harvard U. Administration Building.	Mets notch their first win of the season, 9–5 over the Expos.
April 17	Sirhan Sirhan is convicted of the 1968 murder of Senator Robert Kennedy.	Nemesis Jim Bunning, who pitched a perfect game against the Mets in 1964, blanks them again.
April 19	Armed African American students take over a building at Cornell U.	Tom Seaver bests Bob Gibson in a classic match-up, 2–1.
Apr. 20	Cal-Berkeley students create People's Park as a locus of the antiwar protest movement.	Jerry Grote drives in four runs and Cleon Jones scores four times in an 11–3 romp over the Cardinals.
May 10	The Vietnam battle that inspired the movie *Hamburger Hill* is waged.	Seaver four-hits the Astros as Jones raises his average to .402.
June 1	"Give Peace a Chance" is recorded during John Lennon and Yoko Ono's weeklong "Bed In."	Ron Swoboda literally "walks off" the Giants with a bases-loaded pass in the ninth.
June 3	Seventy-four U.S. sailors are killed when the destroyer *Evans* collides with an Australian vessel.	Two Ed Kranepool homers down the Dodgers, 5–2.
June 8	President Nixon announces a 25,000-troop drawdown in Vietnam.	Seaver dominates the Padres with 14 strikeouts in seven innings.
June 22	The polluted Cuyahoga River in Cleveland catches fire.	Jerry Koosman's 1–0 gem caps a doubleheader sweep of St. Louis.
July 3	Former Rolling Stones guitarist Brian Jones drowns.	Gary Gentry silences the Cardinals, 8–1.
July 8	The first U.S. troops are withdrawn from Vietnam.	Kranepool's two-run single in the ninth caps a come-back for an important win over the first-place Cubs.
July 18	Mary Jo Kopechne dies after Senator Edward Kennedy drives the car in which they were traveling off a bridge on Chappaquiddick Island.	Art Shamsky's home run keys a win over Montreal.
July 20	Neil Armstrong becomes the first man to walk on the moon.	Bobby Pfeil squeezes home the winning run in the tenth inning against the Expos.
August 10	The Manson Family concludes its killing spree of eight people and an unborn child in Los Angeles.	Nolan Ryan leaves a win over the Braves with an injury that sidelines him for nearly a month.
August 13	Four million people line New York City streets to fete the Apollo 11 astronauts.	A loss in Houston leaves the Mets ten games out of first—their biggest deficit of the season.
August 16–17	The Woodstock Festival rocks upstate New York.	The Mets sweep back-to-back doubleheaders against the Padres by scores of 2–0, 2–1, 3–2, and 3–2.
September 2	The first automated teller machine in the U.S. is installed 15 miles away from Shea Stadium.	A Tug McGraw strikeout halts a furious Dodgers ninth-inning rally.
September 26	The Beatles release *Abbey Road* in the United Kingdom.	Koosman hurls the second of four consecutive Mets shutouts.
October 15	Hundreds of thousands participate in the National Moratorium antiwar demonstrations.	The Mets draw within one game of the world championship with a ten-inning win over Baltimore.

The Benevolent Dictator

Gil Hodges (left) had no qualms about yanking Gary Gentry early in Game 3 of the NLCS because he had a "secret weapon" in the bull-pen: Twenty-two-year-old Nolan Ryan came on in relief and limited the Braves to three hits over seven innings.

Nothing Casey Stengel ever said was more sagaciously screwy than when he described the intimidating Gil Hodges's handshake as one that would "squeeze your earbrows off." As a player, the former Dodger combined 370-home-run power at the plate with three-Gold Glove finesse around the first-base bag. The dichotomy translated into a managerial style that cast him as part menacing dictator, part father-confessor (he once talked suicidal Senators pitcher Ryne Duren off a bridge), and part elegant tactician. As a buttress for a Mets edifice that was erected on impressionable youth, the former Marine was the perfect pillar.

On the recommendation of Mets ownership, GM Bing Devine and his assistant, Johnny Murphy, brokered a deal to hire Hodges away from Washington for the 1968 season. Ron Swoboda couldn't believe how abruptly the club's culture changed: "Gil's approach was entirely different from the year before. His approach was serious and all business, man, and he was a big, imposing guy… scared the [bleep] out of you."

Hodges certainly didn't take any "bleep" from Cleon Jones on a July afternoon in 1969 when, after his left fielder lollygagged a play, the skipper called time and strode onto the outfield, where he commanded Jones to sit his lazy "bleep" on the bench. The incident is often cited as having turned the Mets' season around.

In April 1972, following the last round of golf that he planned to play in Florida before heading north to start his fifth season at the Mets' helm, Hodges (a heavy smoker) died of a heart attack. It was two days before his 48th birthday.

"When Gil was running the ballclub, you always felt that things were sane, even if you were kind of insane," recalled Tug McGraw years later. Today, Mets fans are left to ruminate on the insanity of Hodges's exclusion from the Hall of Fame.

The Outbound "Express"

One day in 1964, Mets scout Red Murff visited Alvin, Texas, and after watching the local high school team play, he told the squad's coach that one of his players had "one of the ten best arms in the world." The incredulous skipper named two other players before guessing that Murff was referring to Nolan Ryan. At the time, Ryan weighed all of 140 pounds and had no clue how to properly throw a baseball or where it was going when it left his hand, but his ability to throw the pill preternaturally fast made strikeout victims of 19 batters in one seven-inning high school game. He remained sufficiently underestimated when he was drafted 295th in the 1965 draft and was *still* underestimated when the Mets gave him away six and a half years later.

By 1968, after either walking, hitting, or humiliating virtually every minor-league hitter he faced, Ryan was in the bigs to stay. Broadcaster Ralph Kiner dubbed his fastball the "Ryan Express" after the Sinatra film *Von Ryan's Express*. On the days Nolie could keep his 100-mph fastball in the same zip code as home plate, batters had no chance. In the three games in which he had his most strikeouts as a Met, he fanned 45 while allowing only nine hits in 27 innings. His relief work in 1969—which included a win in the NLCS clincher and a save in Game 3 of the World Series—was vital.

Ryan spent several seasons in and out of the Mets' rotation, failing to convince the club that he'd ever harness his heat. After the '71 campaign, GM Bob Scheffing traded him and three prospects to get Jim Fregosi from California, where Ryan's career as the greatest strikeout pitcher in baseball history got its traction. Fregosi turned out to be a disinterested disaster and was gone in 18 months—sold to the Rangers, for whom Ryan later threw two of his seven no-hitters.

Jim Fregosi, the bust the Mets received in exchange for Nolan Ryan (pictured), may still have been a little sheepish seven years later when he said, "He's not the best pitcher in baseball. Never has been. He's the most exciting .500 pitcher in baseball."

METS MEMORABILIA

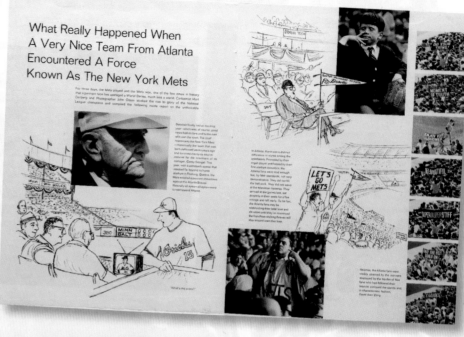

What Really Happened When A Very Nice Team From Atlanta Encountered A Force Known As The New York Mets

TOM SEAVER DIDN'T NEED TO PEN "HOF '92" TO REMIND FOLKS OF HIS HALL OF FAME STATUS. IN HIS INDUCTION SPEECH, HE CALLED GIL HODGES "THE MOST IMPORTANT PART OF MY LIFE FROM A PROFESSIONAL STANDPOINT."

METS MANIA INFILTRATED THE MAINSTREAM IN 1969, AS AMERICANS WERE CAPTIVATED BY THE "MIRACLE" THANKS TO EXPOSURE SUCH AS THIS PIECE FROM *LIFE* MAGAZINE.

SHEA STADIUM TOUR

TOUR STARTS HERE

EVEN AS SHEA STADIUM WAS BEING DEMOLISHED IN 2009, ONE FINAL TOUR WAS ARRANGED FOR FANS. ABOUT 100 SHOWED UP IN POOR WEATHER, MOST DRESSED IN BLUE AND ORANGE, CAMERAS IN HAND, SINGING THE TEAM SONG AND CHANTING "LET'S GO METS!"

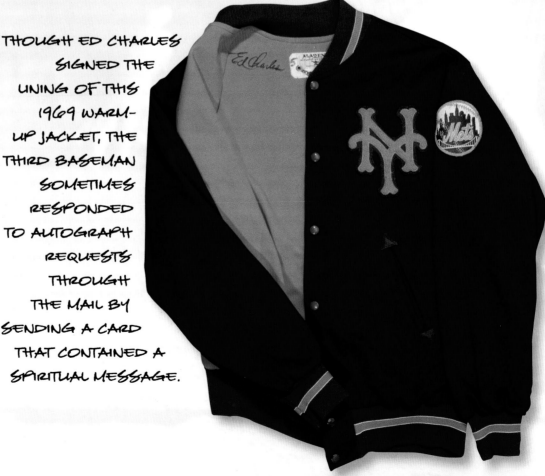

THOUGH ED CHARLES SIGNED THE LINING OF THIS 1969 WARM-UP JACKET, THE THIRD BASEMAN SOMETIMES RESPONDED TO AUTOGRAPH REQUESTS THROUGH THE MAIL BY SENDING A CARD THAT CONTAINED A SPIRITUAL MESSAGE.

DAILY NEWS
NEW YORK'S PICTURE NEWSPAPER ®

FINAL ★★★★

MORE THAN TWICE THE CIRCULATION OF ANY OTHER PAPER IN AMERICA

128   New York, N.Y. 10017, Thursday, April 23, 1970

IT'S K-DAY AT SHEA
Seaver Fans Record 19, 10 in Row

Met Tom Seaver starts to wind up 16th strikeout on hill at Shea yesterday. Seaver struck out Padres' Murrell in eighth with the pitch not before he really twisted him into position to throw. Seaver, took plaque for 1969 Cy Young Award yesterday, pitched a record-breaking game that gave Mets 2-1 victory.

Tom Gave 'Em Clean Air To Swing At

And if the new marks in the record book weren't enough to make the day's pitching worthwhile, Tom's pretty wife, Nancy, adds some incentive. After the game, the kiss, and a TV interview, Seaver went to showers. Tom chalked up new consecutive strikeout record (10) and new day-game record (19).

Story on page 106

TOM SEAVER, PERHAPS THE MOST MECHANICALLY SOUND PITCHER WHO EVER TOED THE RUBBER, WAS INDEED A MACHINE ON APRIL 22, 1970, WHEN HE STRUCK OUT 19 PADRES—INCLUDING THE LAST TEN OF THE GAME. IN THE 2-1 WIN, 96 OF HIS 136 OFFERINGS WERE STRIKES.

JERRY GROTE WAS SUCH A GAMER THAT, WHEN HE WAS THE LAST PLAYER TO TOUCH A BALL IN AN INNING, HE WOULD ROLL IT TO A SPOT WHERE THE OPPOSING PITCHER WOULD HAVE TO WALK THE MAXIMUM DISTANCE TO RETRIEVE IT.

GIL HODGES' PENNANT FEVER

The excitingly realistic baseball game that lets YOU manage real major league teams!

Every player in both the American and National leagues performs as he does in real life... and YOU make the decisions!

RGI

RESEARCH GAMES, INC. USED THE NAME OF GIL HODGES TO PROMOTE THIS PROBABILITY-BASED DICE GAME FOLLOWING THE MIRACLE OF 1969. IT CONTAINED CHARTS AND STRATEGY CARDS INTENDED TO GENERATE REALISTIC PERFORMANCES BY ACTUAL PLAYERS.

Garden of Delights

From the beginning, the Mets' outfield resembled a casting call for the Island of Misfit Toys. It was no different going into 1969, as the club had made no major off-season moves to address the shortcomings of a group that aggregately had batted .228 with scant power the previous season. The candidates all came with patchy resumes that conveyed underachievement, uninspiring athleticism, or unpredictability. From this collage of remnants, however, sprung nothing less than a masterpiece.

At 26, Tommie Agee was already beginning his eighth major-league season, only one of which (his 1966 AL Rookie of the Year effort with the White Sox) had produced results that were commensurate with his innate power and speed. In '68, perhaps spooked by the fastball Bob Gibson stuck in his ear with the first pitch of the Grapefruit League, he was abysmal: He posted a .217 average and hit only five home runs. Tom Seaver proved prescient the next spring when he told writers, "The ballclub has really improved. It all depends on the kind of year number 20 has."

Number 20 had quite the year. Agee hit .271, and his 26 home runs were unheard of from a leadoff hitter of the era. More significantly, his *cirque du soleil* approach to playing center field looked positively Mays-like to nostalgic New Yorkers.

Positioned to Agee's right was his old Mobile, Alabama, boyhood buddy, Cleon Jones. For years, Jones scuffled at the plate and perplexed teammates with his shyness-mistaken-for-surliness, but he seemed to relax when Tommie came aboard in '68; that year, Jones Agee the team with his .297 average and 23 stolen bases. He was not as naturally gifted as Agee, but Jones's confidence and his statistics continued to advance in '69. A student of hitting, Jones made the All-Star team and, at .340, finished behind only Pete Rose and Roberto Clemente in the batting race.

If Agee and Jones were the thoroughbreds in the garden, right-field platooners Ron

Johnny Bench tagged Tommie Agee out on this play in 1970, but just a few weeks earlier, Agee had stolen home for the winning run against the Dodgers in the bottom of the tenth inning.

SWOBODA

This nameplate hung over Ron Swoboda's locker in 1969. Forty years later, the long-time baseball broadcaster was chosen to accept the Thurman Munson Award (which recognizes athletic and community accomplishment) on behalf of the '69 Mets team.

Cleon Jones was talented but enigmatic. It was almost a microcosm of his career when, in the same week in 1971, he hit into a triple play and blasted the 1,000th home run in Mets history.

than a resin bag, it seemed that the hustling Marylander rose to every occasion at the plate and in the field in 1969.

His portside counterpart, Shamsky, was the first—and still the only—player in major-league history to hit three home runs in a game that he didn't start. He achieved this in 1966 when he was playing with the Reds, but his .231 career average as 1969 commenced scarcely guaranteed him a spot on the roster. Shamsky, however, more than earned one by clouting 14 homers and batting .300 (not to mention .538 in the NLCS) in his part-time role.

This quartet, spelled by defensive wizard Rod Gaspar, hardly comprised the prototypical championship-caliber outfield in 1969. It hardly mattered.

Ron Swoboda's max-effort approach to the game made him one of the most popular Mets ever. "I tried to trade four baseball cards for yours," a young fan once wrote to him. "You will surely go to the Hall of Fame. I hope you never die."

"Rocky" Swoboda and Art Shamsky were the old, reliable plowhorses.

Swoboda first captured the imaginations of Mets fans during his 1965 rookie year when he topped the team with 19 longballs (the first of which was estimated to have come to rest 565 feet from home plate) and formed a mutual admiration society with Casey Stengel. "Soboda," or "The People's Cherce" (as Stengel alternately referred to him), was a free spirit and a free swinger, and both inclinations caught up to him to some extent. Though he never matched his '65 home run total and he covered less ground on defense

Big Donn . . .

No trade in franchise history was more crucial than the acquisition of Donn Clendenon in June 1969. That season, 22 of his 37 RBI for the Mets either tied the game or put his club ahead.

Few Mets have ever had as much going for—or against—them as Donn Clendenon.

In mind, body, and spirit, he was extra-large. The Cleveland Browns and Harlem Globetrotters had offered contracts to the 6'4" athlete upon his departure from college, but he opted to sign with the Pittsburgh Pirates and peaked with them in 1966, when he hit .299 with 28 home runs. Three years hence, the first baseman was World Series MVP for the Mets and the player most credited for elevating the team to (or past) its capabilities with his heavy hitting and inspirational personality following his acquisition in June. "Until Donn Clendenon showed up with his big bat, we had no chance of winning anything," recollected Ron Swoboda.

Life imposed itself on "Clink."

. . . and Little Al

In 1968, Al Weis was a throw-in to the Tommie Agee trade, coveted by the Mets wholly because of his proficiency as a second baseman and shortstop. While it's unsurprising that the slight Long Islander "muscled up" for only five home runs in his four seasons as a Met (one came in the World Series), his trio of dingers in 1969 are among the most crucial in team annals. "Don't try to make me out as a home run hitter," said Weis at the time. "In fact, I'm not even a hitter." Considering that his .219 career batting average is one of the 15 lowest ever by players who have appeared in at least 800 games, he had a point.

In a way, Al Weis's brilliant World Series play was a measure of revenge. Two years earlier, Orioles star Frank Robinson had torn up the second baseman's knee with a hard slide, ending Weis's season in June.

He was six months old when his father died; his stepfather (Nish Williams, a former Negro Leagues player) withheld allowance if he practiced his baseball insufficiently. Clendenon taught school before he ever signed a pro contract and, during off-seasons, worked as a detective and a restaurateur while pursuing a law degree. Following his playing days, he practiced law, became CEO of two companies, battled cocaine addiction, fought leukemia for more than a decade, earned certification in drug counseling, and wrote a book.

In a way, the Mets were a footnote to Donn Clendenon, but to the Mets, he was a chapter all his own.

MMMM Good

"**M**" stood for Mets mediocrity during the first seven seasons of the 1970s, when the club won between 82 and 86 games in each year but '74 (when they barely avoided the basement). But the letter also represented a quartet of outstanding—if unappreciated—players.

Jim McAndrew established his rep as the unluckiest Met ever when neither his teammates nor foes scored more than two runs in eight of his first nine big-league starts in 1968. Four years later, his career ERA read 3.31, yet he'd lost eight more decisions than he'd won.

Jon Matlack's fate was similar: His career ledger was a mere 82–81 despite a 3.03 ERA. At times, the future minor-league pitching coach was the best lefty in the league—he was the 1972 NL Rookie of the Year, made three All-Star teams, and spun more Mets shutouts (26) than anyone save Tom Seaver and Jerry Koosman.

Runs were as scarce as Yankee fans at Shea Stadium during this decade, so John "Hammer" Milner's 20-homer seasons in 1973 and '74 seemed positively Ruthian. Injuries, bad personal habits, and the inability to hit the crooked pitches crippled his career thereafter.

No more professional player and no finer defensive second baseman has graced the franchise rolls than Felix Millan. He was butter turning the double play, twice neared 200 hits, and rarely struck out.

His hometown of Lost Nation, Iowa, declared Jim McAndrew Day to fete the Mets pitcher after the 1969 World Series. (A berg of fewer than 500 folks, Lost Nation had a town marshal in the 1940s with the unfortunate name Toad Butt.)

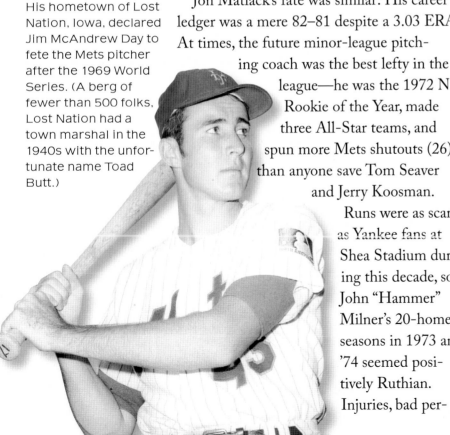

The Second Coming

The most eminent "M" in team history arrived in 1972, when Willie Mays was procured from San Francisco after the Giants snubbed his demands for a long-term contract. On May 14, amidst "Say Hey" hysteria, Mays made his Mets debut and cranked a key homer against his former Giants teammates. At 41, Willie had little left to offer save memories, but he hit like crazy at first, sparking the Mets to an 11-game winning streak. For a few weeks, it was 1954 again.

Willie Mays was acquired for pitcher Charlie Williams and 50 grand on May 11, 1972. When the club ran off 11 straight wins and the revered center fielder batted .348 in his first 14 games, *Sports Illustrated* pronounced the Mets "AMaysing."

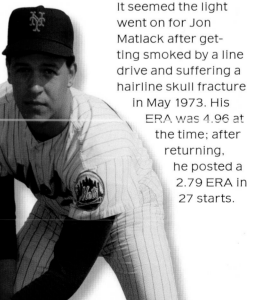

It seemed the light went on for Jon Matlack after getting smoked by a line drive and suffering a hairline skull fracture in May 1973. His ERA was 4.96 at the time; after returning, he posted a 2.79 ERA in 27 starts.

Something to Believe In

From the moment Cleon Jones squeezed the fly ball that ended the 1969 World Series, the Mets were a changed team. They got a little famous; they had a little money; they got a little cocky. Yes, they were winners, but they were no longer Amazin' and by no means miraculous.

Some of them showed up at spring training in 1970 out of shape from a winter of revelry and rubber chicken. Manager Gil Hodges decried the lack of cohesion, and his heavy-handed style suddenly rankled more than it motivated. In '71, personnel turnover accelerated, and just before the '72 season opened, Hodges passed away. He was replaced by Yogi Berra, whom the players liked far more than respected. The upshot was that in the three seasons after the championship, the Mets contended into midseason before fading to identical win totals of 83 each year.

It was in this fog of inertia that the 1973 campaign got underway and, deep into the summer, there was no sign of the team's ennui lifting. Every week seemed to bring a new injury or a ripe controversy, and rumors persisted that Berra would be fired. After one dispiriting loss, M. Donald Grant broke out one of his rah-rah speeches to the troops. Most players thought these periodic homilies by the team chairman were farcical, but this time Tug McGraw—the most emotive of all Mets—suddenly rose to his feet and shouted,

"The AMaysing Mets" heralded a *Sports Illustrated* cover when the club caught fire after acquiring Mays in 1972. Behind the scenes, however, the proud legend fretted over his injuries and inability to perform to his standards.

A celebratory Tom Seaver beat the Reds in the decisive fifth game of the 1973 NLCS to clinch the Mets' second pennant. He would pitch another 13 years but would never again notch a postseason victory.

"That's right, Mr. Grant, ya gotta believe!" The riled-up reliever bounced from teammate to teammate, exhorting, "Do you believe? Ya gotta believe!"

What the players *believed* was that McGraw had come unglued and that he would soon be traded for mocking the boss. It was, to the contrary, a transformative moment. Provoked by McGraw's cheerleading from the bullpen, the fans soon took up the cry, and chants of "Ya gotta believe!" swept Shea and echoed throughout New York.

Nonetheless, it wasn't until August 31 that the Mets extricated themselves from last place for good. Fortunately, St. Louis stood only two games above .500 and five and a half games ahead of New York. "It's beginning to feel like 1969 all over again," chirped Jerry Koosman.

In many ways, it was. September played out like a climb up a playground slide slathered in baby oil, but inspired by McGraw (5–0 with 12 saves in his last 19 appearances), the team went 20–8 to edge the Cardinals and earn the right to face Cincinnati in the NLCS. A five-game dismissal of the soon-to-be Big Red Machine—during which the New York pitching staff posted a sparkling 1.33 ERA—made the 82–79 Mets the "worst team" ever to win a pennant.

There was a suspension of disbelief when the 1973 club drew to within one victory of becoming the unlikeliest of world champs. Their bats went cold, however, and the Mets dropped the next two games to the A's.

Willie Mays lost the final contest of his career in the 1973 World Series, but in Game 2, he drove in the go-ahead run in the 12th inning.

New York's World Series opponents were the maverick, mustachioed Oakland A's. Profound underdogs, the Mets spoiled great pitching from Jon Matlack in Game 1 and Tom Seaver in Game 3 with defensive gaffes but salvaged a sloppy Game 2 that included Willie Mays's final career hit. Matlack and Jerry Koosman stopped the A's cold in Games 4 and 5, respectively, to pull the Mets to within a game of the crown, but Oakland scuffled back to take Games 6 and 7.

It was a disappointing conclusion, but considering the discontent brewing inside the organization and the modest composition of the team itself, the 1973 season seemed almost like a gift. Fans did well to savor it because, for the entire decade that lay ahead, they were given little to believe in.

METS MEMORABILIA

THIS 1973 NATIONAL LEAGUE CHAMPIONSHIP RING BELONGED TO JERRY GROTE, WHOSE 1969 WORLD SERIES VERSION WAS SOLD BY A MEMORABILIA DEALER FOR $67,500. (IN 2008, DUFFY DYER, GROTE'S BACKUP, HAD HIS SERIES RING STOLEN DURING A VISIT TO THE DOMINICAN REPUBLIC.)

IN HIS FINAL SEASON, WILLIE MAYS BATTED ONLY .211 FOR THE 1973 METS, BUT HE HAD THE HONOR OF SIGNING THE SWEET SPOT ON THIS TEAM BALL. IN A MEASURE OF NOSTALGIC JUSTICE, HE GOT THE FIRST HIT OF THE WORLD SERIES.

WILLIE MAYS SIGNED THIS JERSEY ON THE LEFT SHOULDER, BUT TRUE METS NUMEROLOGISTS KNOW HE WASN'T THE ONLY HALL OF FAMER TO WEAR #24 FOR THE TEAM—RICKEY HENDERSON WAS THE OTHER.

"YOU GOTTA BELIEVE"

WE'RE NUMBER ONE

New York Mets

1973 CHAMPIONS

MIRACLE METS

THIS PENNANT FROM 1973 WAS AS GARISH AS IT WAS PREMATURE. THE METS, OF COURSE, WERE NOT "CHAMPIONS," AS IT IMPLIES.

THIS CAP WAS SIGNED BY JERRY KOOSMAN, WHO WAS A 20-GAME WINNER AND 20-GAME LOSER IN BACK-TO-BACK SEASONS. OVERALL, KOOZ WAS A GREAT MET WHO TIED THE NL ROOKIE RECORD WITH SEVEN SHUTOUTS IN 1968, MADE TWO ALL-STAR TEAMS, AND WENT 4-0 IN THE POSTSEASON.

YOU GOTTA
Beee-leeeevvvve
NEW YORK METS

A TEAM THAT STOOD 11 1/2 GAMES OUT OF FIRST PLACE ON AUGUST 5 SOON HAD ALL OF METDOM BEEE-LEEEEVVVVING IN 1973. NEW YORK WAS SATURATED WITH SYMBOLS OF SOLIDARITY SUCH AS THIS CHEESY BUMPER STICKER.

THOUSANDS OF FANS BESIEGED THE FIELD MOMENTS AFTER THE METS CLINCHED THE 1969 WORLD SERIES. "THE FANS WERE COMING OVER THE TOP OF THE DUGOUT," REMEMBERED JERRY KOOSMAN. "THEY WERE FALLING ON TOP OF EACH OTHER...YOU HAD TO WALK OVER THE TOP OF THEM TO GET TO THE CLUBHOUSE."

FINAL

★★★

DAILY NEWS
NEW YORK'S PICTURE NEWSPAPER ®

Vol. 51. No. 98

New York, N.Y. 10017, Friday, October 17, 1969*

WEATHER: Fair, breezy, very cool.

8¢

10¢ OUTSIDE I.I. AND SUBURBS

WORLD CHAMPS!

10 Amazin' Pages on How the Mets Plucked the Birds

NEWS photo by Dan Farrell

"Screwball"

Tug McGraw pitched and lived like there was no tomorrow. He was a bushy-tailed 20-year-old when he arrived in 1965, "dumb" enough to forget his cap on his first road trip and his shoes on his second—and way too "dumb" to know he wasn't supposed to be the first Met ever to beat Sandy Koufax.

Although his career as a starter stalled, McGraw began his run as the Mets' best-ever relief pitcher when he mastered the screwball (the appropriate title of his autobiography) in 1969. He was at the peak of his powers in '71 and '72, when he won 19 games, saved 35 more, and compiled a 1.70 ERA. After a slow start in '73, McGraw emboldened himself, his team, and all of New York with his "Ya Gotta Believe" mantra, which helped catalyze a so-so team to the World Series.

Fans delighted in the caffeinated lefty's demonstrative approach to the game, which included his trademark ritual of slapping glove to thigh after recording big outs. And few other players could get away with his outrageous quotes. Asked one spring what he was going to do with his hefty raise, McGraw responded, "Ninety percent of it I'll spend on good times, women, and Irish whiskey. The other 10 percent I'll waste." Asked whether he had a preference for pitching on AstroTurf or grass, he replied, "I don't know. I've never smoked AstroTurf."

At 22, McGraw fathered a boy who he didn't acknowledge until 18 years later. The two became close after that, and when his

dad was dying of brain cancer, Tim McGraw released a country album that would win two Grammy Awards; the title song related the pitcher's final confessional and a prayer for his son: "Some day, I hope you get the chance to live like you were dyin'." In 2004, at age 59, there were no more tomorrows for Tug, but he bequeathed Mets fans a lifetime of amazin' yesterdays.

"The 1969 season was like being in love—you always remember the first time," Tug McGraw once recalled. However, the passionate reliever is best remembered for '73, when he decreed, "Ya gotta believe!"

Mini-Met

Watching him play, it sometimes seemed as if Bud Harrelson's outsized heart would burst right through the "S" on the Superman T-shirt he always wore under his jersey. The skeletal shortstop had difficulty staying above 150 pounds and healthy, but until Jose Reyes came along in 2003, he sustained 30 years of recognition as the undisputed finest of all Mets at the position.

Harrelson manned short for much of 11 seasons, but one play defined him. In Game 3 of the 1973 NLCS, Pete Rose barreled into him during a double play, and then threw an elbow on his way up. After Harrelson cussed him out, the two wrestled and the benches emptied. So incensed were fans at Shea that one of them threw an empty liquor bottle at Rose during the next inning, which caused the Reds to pull their defense off the field. "I might have been small and frail-looking," said Harrelson, "but I was never afraid."

Born, appropriately, on D-Day, it was Harrelson's "D" that kept him in the majors all those years. His smooth, intrepid glovework won him two invitations to the All-Star Game and a 1971 Gold Glove Award. At the plate...suffice it to disclose that while Rose is baseball's all-time hits leader, Harrelson holds the "record" for fewest knocks by a shortstop who's appeared in 1,500 or more games.

Harrelson retired after the 1980 season (he'd been traded by New York following the 1977 campaign) and became a coach with the Mets in 1982. He was the team's third-base coach in 1986, and he was the only man to be on the field for both of the franchise's world championships. As a player, coach, and manager (a position to which he was named in 1990), no one has worn the Mets uniform in more games.

Wispy Bud Harrelson had a tendency to lose 20 or more pounds over the course of a season, but his daring dust-up with Pete Rose is regarded as the weightiest play of the 1973 NLCS.

CHAPTER THREE

THE LOST DECADE
1974–1983

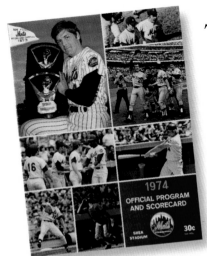

Nothing about the 1974 season resembled the surprising, sublime success of '73. Even Tom Seaver (upper left, showing off his '73 Cy Young Award) faltered to his first non-winning season (11–11).

THE DECADE THAT lasted from 1974 to '83 was more about penance than pennants. The Mets had a lot to atone for—a failure of ownership, ineffectual management, the trade of an icon, and a dizzying string of losing seasons that made this era seem like 1962 all over again (but without the charm). Mercifully, the moribund franchise was sold, and though the patient's pulse remained faint, it showed some vital signs.

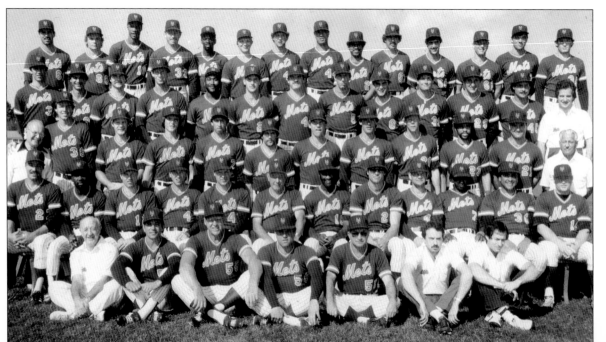

The proud Mets franchise hit rock bottom with this 1983 team, which finished last for the fifth time in seven years. They scored the fewest runs in the league and didn't have a starting pitcher with a winning record. But hope, and wins, weren't far on the horizon.

Tom Seaver was unhappy with a call in a start against the Pirates on September 1, 1975, but most everything went his way that day. His four-hit, ten-strikeout shutout produced his 20th win en route to his third and final Cy Young Award.

The Mets Experience

Like the city under their feet, Mets fans have a certain grittiness to them. Pulitzer Prize-winning columnist Jimmy Breslin once called the Amazins "the team for every guy who has to get out of bed in the morning and go to work for short money on a job he does not like." It was this commonality that superseded the societal forces that otherwise might have driven those folks apart, and it was the timelessness of baseball itself that unified them.

Portions of the New York demographic—the more well-to-do (but less baseball-impassioned) neighborhoods and the artsier nooks of Manhattan, for example—were Yankee strongholds in the 1960s and '70s. A far greater segment of the populace, however, shared affinity with the Mets, no matter how fractionalized by geography, race, culture,

Hgt. 6'-6" Wt. 210
Birth Date 12/21/48

Born: Pendleton, Ore.

© MAJOR LEAGUE BASEBALL PLAYERS ASSOC. 1976

DAVE KINGMAN INFIELDER

NEW YORK METS

In 1977, fast-food knockoff Burger Chef served its kids "Funmeals" in trays that featured punch-out discs of baseball players. It was said of irascible Dave Kingman that he'd sooner punch you out than look at you.

The catchphrase of New York Mayor Ed Koch (shown here throwing out a first pitch at Shea in 1978) was "How'm I doing?" The dreadful Mets of the era would have been afraid to ask that question.

or economics. In the Bronx during the '70s, standards of living got lower as high-rises got higher; gangs ruled the streets; a wave of arson spread through the borough; and the population was in decline for only the second time since 1800. Owing to this, residents began flocking to airy Staten Island. Life in Queens (where Shea Stadium was located) seemed something like the insulated existence portrayed in *All in the Family*, the hit sitcom of the time; conversely, Brooklyn was one of the most ethnically diverse locales on the planet. But when the Mets were created, wrote George Vecsey of *The New York Times*, "People who would sneer at each other in the subways or in a bar began talking to each other in the Polo Grounds."

In those early days, Mets fans even acquired an appellation of their own: "The New Breed." Its skin thickened by the escape of the Dodgers and Giants and its humility honed by years of hammerings on the field, The New Breed came to relish the successes of 1969 and 1973 in the manner of a family permitted to buy dinner at The Rainbow Room with food stamps. Yankee loyalists ate (metaphorically, anyway) at Toots Shor's in Manhattan, which Yogi Berra perceived was "so popular that nobody goes there anymore"; the Mets faithful, on the other hand, grabbed a "sour" at Guss' Pickles, a "slice" from the corner pizza stand, a Rheingold (beer) at the local watering hole, or a "Coney Island" (hot dog) at the ballgame.

During Shea's first decade, the Mets' average attendance was almost exactly two million per season—about 10,000 spectators per game above the major-league norm and about a half-million more than the Yanks. However, their Mettle would be sorely tested: Following the pennant win of 1973, the club fell to 20 games under .500 in 1974, rebounded modestly for third-place finishes in each of the next two seasons, then devolved into a laughingstock by finishing with winning percentages no higher than .420 from 1977 to 1983. As hardy as the fans had proven to be, attendance plunged commensurately—and it wasn't just because losing was no longer quaint. The franchise's detached and miserly front office seemed to make it their business to antagonize The New Breed. The roster lacked star power; the players lacked passion. Suddenly, Shea was no longer a fun place to be. The Mets were fortunate simply to be *noticed* by their fans; expecting them to spend their "short money" on a ticket required a special kind of temerity.

In a 1978 season that provided little to cheer about, Doug Flynn's work around the second-base bag was an exception. He and Edgardo Alfonzo share the club's position record for career fielding percentage at .987.

It was perhaps a lack of star power that prompted the team to put its logo, as opposed to the traditional player photos, on the cover of its 1979 official yearbook. Joel Youngblood led Joe Torre's 63–99 unit with a mere 16 homers, and only one pitcher (Craig Swan) won more than six games.

An Unholy Trinity

Mrs. Joan Payson died on October 4, 1975, and with her went a large measure of the Mets' heart. Ownership of the franchise passed to her husband, Charles, who treated it like a Christmas fruitcake. He delegated oversight of the organization to his daughter, Lorinda de Roulet, a sweet lady who once ordered her staff to scurry around the stadium and collect foul balls to be reused. She, in turn, allowed M. Donald Grant to operate the baseball end with his own special brand of ham-handed futility. The product on the field suffered almost instantly.

"We couldn't do anything because the man wouldn't let the purse strings go," recalled Joe Pignatano, a Mets coach from 1968 to 1981. "The man I'm talking about is Mr. Payson.

Charles Payson—the husband of team owner Joan—was reclusive until the Mets won it all in 1969. Six years to the day after New York played its first post-season game, his wife died, leaving the club in his disinterested hands.

We had some bad teams and we had no money. Mrs. de Roulet tried, but the old man wouldn't let go of the money."

Not that Grant wanted to spend it. Just as baseball was entering the age of free agency and new Yankees owner George Steinbrenner was itching to buy himself a championship or six, Grant entrenched himself in arrogance: He openly regarded the players as minions and routinely referred to them—without a hint of irony—as his "boys." By 1978, there was not one player from the '73 title team left in the starting lineup, and only Jerry Koosman remained from the club's vaunted pitching staff. The once-vibrant confines of Shea had become known, sardonically, as "Grant's Tomb." The cryptkeeper was fired in 1978 after a second straight last-place finish, but it would take years to roll back the stone.

Chairman M. Donald Grant played a major role in building the 1969 championship team, but his refusal to adapt his high-handed management style tore the team apart over the next decade.

The "Midnight Massacre"

June 15, 1977, was the franchise's darkest hour, and it was M. Donald Grant who shot out the lights.

The Mets chairman had once before tried to trade Tom Seaver, only to relent amidst a maelstrom of public outrage. This time, however, he was determined to get it done rather than fairly compensate the iconic pitcher, who was making one-third the salary that Reggie Jackson pulled in across town. Seaver was infuriated by Grant's intransigence. "He didn't like me and I didn't like him," Seaver recollected. "One day he called me a communist."

At one point, the star went over Grant's head to Lorinda de Roulet and struck a deal,

At one point during Tom Seaver's interviews with reporters on the day he was traded, he was so choked up that he borrowed a pad and pencil so he could write down his answer to a question.

but when *New York Daily News* columnist Dick Young (who shared Grant's plantation mentality) disparaged Seaver and insulted his wife, Nancy, the pitcher backed out of the agreement. He demanded a trade and got it—to Cincinnati, for four fair-to-middlin' players.

Grant (henceforth known simply as Judas to fans) didn't stop there. On that same evening, he dealt Dave Kingman to San Diego for a pair of fringe major-leaguers (one of whom was future Mets manager Bobby Valentine) rather than pay market value for the team's only marquee bat. The roster had been eviscerated, and that old familiar feeling of violation cascaded over the fan base once again.

Three days later, Seaver spun a three-hit shutout for the Reds. His old team lost 63 of its last 100 games as a new Yankees dynasty commenced across town. The Mets would never truly own New York again.

METS MEMORABILIA

A POPULAR METS GIVEAWAY IN THE 1970S WAS THE ANNUAL PHOTO ALBUM (SUCH AS THIS ONE FROM '77), WHICH WAS IDEAL FOR AUTOGRAPH SEEKERS.

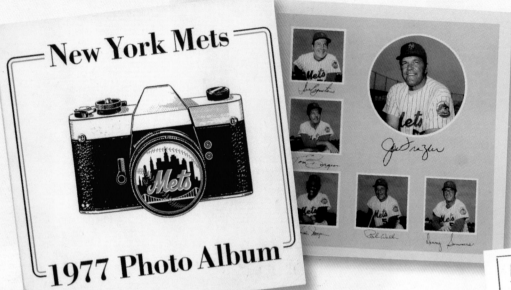

New York Mets

1977 Photo Album

COULD THESE BE THE ONLY FIVE HAPPY PEOPLE IN NEW YORK? THE "MIDNIGHT MASSACRE" TRADES THAT EXILED TOM SEAVER AND DAVE KINGMAN NETTED MANAGER JOE TORRE (CENTER) NEW OPERATIVES (FROM LEFT) DOUG FLYNN, PAT ZACHRY, STEVE HENDERSON, AND BOBBY VALENTINE.

CARDINALS AND METS
at Al Lang Stadium, St. Petersburg
Combined Schedule — 1978

11	Cardinals vs. Mets
12	Mets vs. Cardinals
13	Phillies vs. Cardinals
14	Minnesota vs. Mets
15	Toronto vs. Mets
16	Detroit vs. Mets
	Atlanta vs. Cardinals
	Yankees vs. Mets
	Cincinnati vs. Mets
(N)	Toronto vs. Cardinals
(N)	Mets vs. Cardinals
(N)	Cincinnati vs. Mets
	Los Angeles vs. Mets
	Boston vs. Cardinals
	Minnesota vs. Cardinals
	Detroit vs. Mets
(N)	Pittsburgh vs. Mets
	Cardinals vs. Mets
(N)	Baltimore vs. Cardinals
	Cincinnati vs. Cardinals
(N)	Phillies vs. Mets
	White Sox vs. Mets
	Kansas City vs. Mets
	Atlanta vs. Cardinals
(N)	Cardinals vs. Mets

MAJOR LEAGUE BASEBALL
MARCH 11 THROUGH APRIL 4, 1978

ST. LOUIS **CARDINALS**	NEW YORK **METS**

AL LANG STADIUM — St. Petersburg, Fla.

Box and Loge Box seats may be purchased in advance for all games at the Al Lang Stadium Box Office which will be open daily from 10:00 A.M. to 4:00 P.M. starting Mon., February 20.

Bleacher Seats $1.00   Grandstand Seats $2.00
Field and Loge Boxes $3.25

DAY GAMES 1:30 P.M.
(N) NIGHT GAMES 7:30 P.M.

PHONE RESERVATIONS 894-4773
82

8 ♥

Dave Kingman
outfield, 1975-1977, 1981-1983

Big time slugger: in each of his three full years as a Met, posted a top 10 season for home runs

8 ♥

KINGMAN, SHOWN HERE AS PART OF HERODECK!'S SET OF PLAYING CARDS, COULD BE A JOKER, BUT HE WON HEARTS BY "DIALING 8" FOR NUMEROUS LONG-DISTANCE HOME RUNS. HIS RATE OF ONE DINGER PER 15.1 AT-BATS IS THE BEST IN CLUB ANNALS.

AL LANG STADIUM IN ST. PETERSBURG WAS THE METS' SPRING-TRAINING HOME FROM 1962 TO '87. THINGS WERE GRIM THERE IN '78, WITH THE TEAM BESET BY PLAYER DISCONTENT WITH MANAGEMENT. THIRD BASEMAN LENNY RANDLE EVEN STAGED A TWO-DAY "RETIREMENT."

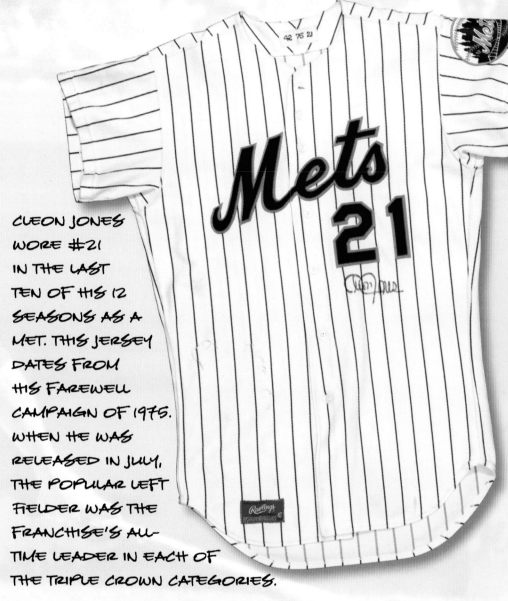

THE CITY BREATHED EASIER WHEN MASS MURDERER DAVID BERKOWITZ WAS APPREHENDED IN THE SUMMER OF 1977. ELEVEN DAYS AFTER THE "SON OF SAM" ARREST, EXHALATIONS TURNED TO CHEERS FOR THE RETURN OF TOM SEAVER TO SHEA. METS FANS WERE NEVER SO HAPPY TO LOSE AS THEIR EXILED HERO STRUCK OUT 11 IN A 5-1 REDS VICTORY.

CLEON JONES WORE #21 IN THE LAST TEN OF HIS 12 SEASONS AS A MET. THIS JERSEY DATES FROM HIS FAREWELL CAMPAIGN OF 1975. WHEN HE WAS RELEASED IN JULY, THE POPULAR LEFT FIELDER WAS THE FRANCHISE'S ALL-TIME LEADER IN EACH OF THE TRIPLE CROWN CATEGORIES.

THE METS WEREN'T EXACTLY A HOT TICKET IN 1977, FALLING TO 64-98 AND THE FIRST OF THREE CONSECUTIVE BASEMENT FINISHES. ATTENDANCE SUNK TO ITS LOWEST POINT SINCE THE INAUGURAL SEASON AND WOULDN'T RECOVER UNTIL '84.

Swan's Sad Song

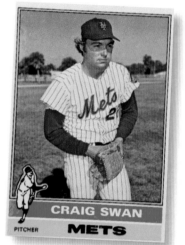

CRAIG SWAN
PITCHER METS

Above: Oft-injured 12-year Met Craig Swan was a fine pitcher for whom something always went wrong. The Mets won only 79 of his 184 starts and were defeated 54 times when he allowed three or fewer earned runs. **Above right:** Injury and his teammates' ineptitude made Craig Swan one of the most unappreciated figures in Mets history. From 1976 to '82, he posted the league's 17th-best ERA, but recorded just its 71st-most wins.

Numerous injuries (he once pitched with an undiagnosed broken arm) and incapable teammates condemned Swan to a 59–71 record for the Mets, but his ERA from 1976 to 1982 was a sharp 3.33. He led the NL in that category with a 2.43 mark in '78, but he recorded only one win in his first 16 starts. Swannie pitched all but five of his 1,235.7 major league innings in a Mets uniform. He probably would have been better off in a different one.

At the precise moment in 1972 that Craig Swan was signing his Mets contract, a lightning bolt struck a tree outside his hotel room window and blasted it into toothpicks. It was an omen that suggested that, from then on, he'd have to accept the bad with the good.

The former Arizona State pitching phenom made it to New York the next season, but after being shelled by the Phillies in his debut, the young hurler overheard M. Donald Grant tell someone to "send that fat kid back to Tidewater." Swan, who admitted to eating a one-pound bag of M&Ms per day during one period in his life, never gained control of his weight. But when he came back from Triple-A to stay in 1976, he shaped up as an ace.

Trade Bait

The significance of another former Arizona State star, Hubie Brooks, is that the Mets couldn't have acquired Gary Carter from Montreal in December 1984 without including him in the deal. After four so-so campaigns, the third baseman put together his first truly good season in 1984, when he homered 16 times and showed enough potential to tantalize the Expos. That year, Brooks also fashioned a 24-game hitting streak, which stood as the club's co-record until 2007. He ultimately fashioned a solid 15-year major-league career, which included a one-year return to Shea in 1991.

Hubie Brooks played in two All-Star Games and won a pair of Silver Sluggers while toiling for Montreal, but none of the other three players the Mets traded for Gary Carter ever achieved substantial major-league success.

Not Just Another Pretty Face

In the diamond dreams of New Yorkers, Lee Mazzilli was a medley of the city's greatest athletic hits—the power of Rocky Graziano (Mazzilli's father was a pro boxer), the speed of Willie Mays (he stole seven bases in a seven-inning minor-league game), the handsomeness of Mickey Mantle, and the ethnic intrigue of Joe DiMaggio. The Brooklyn native—who was selected by the Mets in the first round of the 1973 draft—never approached that paradigm, but one couldn't tell it from his Q rating in Mets Nation.

Dubbed "The Italian Stallion" during the *Rocky*-infatuated '70s, Maz teased stardom early on—he and future Hall of Famer Joe Morgan were the only players in baseball to amass at least 50 homers, 100 steals, and 300 walks between 1977 and 1980. "You can compare him to Pete Rose," gushed Mets batting coach Dick Sisler at the time. "Both are switch hitters, they use the whole field, and they can beat you a number of ways."

Injuries and a weak throwing arm, however, helped to cast Mazzilli as a journeyman by the early '80s. In August 1986, he rejoined the Mets as a valuable pinch-hitter and a teammate of standout pitcher Ron Darling, the man for whom he'd been traded four years earlier.

Since his retirement as a player, Mazzilli's rich post-playing resume has included stints as the Baltimore Orioles manager, a coach, a

This is Lee Mazzilli's second Topps card, issued in 1978. He shared his rookie card of the prior year with three other players, one of whom—Jack Clark—became one of the biggest Mets nemeses of all time.

A Pair of New Yorkers

Both Lee Mazzilli and Joe Torre were heroes of Brooklyn's Italian American community during their shared Mets tenure from 1977 to '81. But while Mazzilli's trade to Texas was virtually an international crisis, nothing about Torre's stint as Mets manager foreshadowed his future success across town. Hired initially as a player-manager after Joe Frazier was fired during the 1977 season, he shuffled substandard personnel for five seasons, none of which produced a winner. The paths of Mazzilli and Torre would cross again, however—from 2000 to '03 and again in '06, Torre employed Maz as a coach with the Yankees.

broadcaster, a Manhattan sports café proprietor, and an off-Broadway actor. His baseball career wasn't exactly the *magnum opus* it once promised to be, but it was a resounding commercial success.

The Web site UltimateMets.com lists the team's players by popularity according to the number of hits on their names. Twenty years after the last game of his modest career, Lee Mazzilli still ranked fifth.

Buying a Fixer-Upper

Lorinda de Roulet, unable to sustain the legacy of her mother (Joan Payson) and embarrassed about bleeding the bank account of her father (Charles Payson), had had enough. After the 1978 season, she pried the toxic hands of M. Donald Grant from the operational buttons. It was too little, too late. After her attempt to lure free agent Pete Rose failed, the Mets blundered to a third consecutive last-place finish, and attendance plummeted to an all-time low—30 percent of what that the team drew at the start of the decade. There was no other option but to put the team up for sale.

A pair of native New Yorkers—Fred Wilpon and Nelson Doubleday Jr.—purchased the team in 1980. Unlike his direct predecessors, Wilpon (a teammate of Sandy Koufax in high school) understood and loved the game; he was positioned as the CEO and the public face of the organization. The reclusive Doubleday never said much—even up until he sold his half of the club to Wilpon in 2002—but the publishing magnate had financed the transformation of the New York

Fred Wilpon's cash and enthusiasm gradually breathed life back into the franchise in the 1980s. He remains the team's owner today.

The Return of the King

There were many reasons Seaver's return in 1983 tugged at the heartstrings of New Yorkers. After he finished his warmups prior to his Opening Day start, he walked to the right-field corner of the stands and handed the ball to a handicapped boy.

"And pitching, number 41 . . ." More than 48,000 voices nearly rendered the next two words inaudible, but when the public address announcer intoned, "Tom . . . Seaver" on Opening Day 1983, Shea Stadium partied like it was 1969.

The Mets had reacquired their prince of pitching from Cincinnati during the off-season, and though it was more of an olive branch to their fans than a warning blast over the heads of competitors, it portended better days in Flushing Meadows. Seaver, then 38, was just average by that point, but he blanked the Phillies for six innings in his return. A year later he would be gone again, lost to the White Sox in the free agent compensation draft.

Islanders from hockey's laughingstock into Stanley Cup winners and aimed to work similar magic with the Mets. This transformation would take time and money. *Lots* of time and money.

Second Scrappers

The Mets once went 33 years without placing a second baseman on the National League All-Star team, and only two of the team's second sackers—Ron Hunt and Edgardo Alfonzo—have ever made it. But that's not to say that the keystone position in New York has always been manned by bums—historically, what the team's second basemen have offered has had far more to do with heart than home runs, key cases in point being Doug Flynn and Wally Backman.

Flynn was part of the proceeds of the much-loathed Tom Seaver trade, which meant he'd be judged unsympathetically. It wasn't long, however, before New York fans cherished his hustle and his nifty work with the leather. In his four-plus years with the Mets, the flimsy Kentuckian batted a meek .234, but in 1980, he earned what is still the only second base Gold Glove in franchise annals.

After the 1981 season, Flynn was dealt to open a spot for Backman, an audacious 22-year-old who, while not as deft in the field, was a far more dangerous offensive weapon. Just as dangerous was his personality: The 5'9" switch-hitter wrestled—and beat—6'6"

Exceptional talent and good baseball instincts were hard for the Mets to come by in the late '70s. Doug Flynn provided the latter despite lacking the former. "I could make a good team better, but I was not good enough to carry a bad team."

teammate Darryl Strawberry (who denounced him as "a little redneck"), cursed opposing players, went to bed filthy, and woke up prepared to clean someone's clock. But no one played harder to win—third baseman Howard Johnson stated that his "drive went off the Richter scale." Backman led the Mets with his gumption for almost a decade, batting .300 twice and stealing 30 bases twice.

Backman's bellicosity may have sparked him to excellence on the ballfield, but his inability to modulate it cost him a nice job. Following the 2004 season, he was hired as manager of the Arizona Diamondbacks, only to be fired four days later after reports of his unpredictable behavior, legal woes, and financial entanglements surfaced.

While managing in the minors, Wally Backman nearly died from a spider bite and had to have a chunk of his scalp removed. As a player, his head was always in the game—his take-no-prisoners style was synonymous with the 1986 Mets.

Recycled Rippers

Even when they were good, the Mets didn't score much; when they were bad in the '70s and early '80s, they might not have scored at all had it not been for deals that netted them two of the game's better hitters.

Rusty Staub (a.k.a. *Le Grand Orange*) arrived in 1972 after five straight All-Star seasons with the Houston Astros and the Montreal Expos. The redhead's unaffected charisma and knack for delivering the clutch knock quickly made him one of the franchise's most beloved players. In 1973, the slugging *saucier* (he ran a popular restaurant on the Upper East Side) slugged three homers in the NLCS and hit .423 in the World Series. In '75, he became the first Met to drive in 100 runs in a season.

A walk-off, pinch-hit jack against the Phillies in 1984 made Rusty Staub the second player (with Ty Cobb) to homer as both a teen and a 40-year-old. Two years later, he became the fourth inductee into the Mets Hall of Fame.

Prior to that '75 season, the Mets purchased Dave Kingman from the Giants. His was a different case altogether. The 6'6" tower of power, Mets announcer Ralph Kiner once advised, "can hit them out of any park, including Yellowstone." Former Met Richie Ashburn also noted that if Kingman's mitt ever needed repair, they'd need to call a welder. Kingman's defensive gracelessness and lofty strikeout totals were only part of his problem—he was an equal-opportunity jerk to teammates, media, and fans alike. No one liked him, but they all liked to watch him hit—he crushed 82 home runs in just over two seasons as a Met and started the All-Star Game in 1976.

Staub was traded after the '75 campaign and Kingman was dealt two years later, but both returned in '81—as a pinch-hitter and first baseman, respectively. In '83, Staub stroked 24 pinch hits (one shy of the then-MLB record). Kingman reached two milestones in '82: He was the first Met to lead the NL in homers (37), and his .204 average was the lowest ever by a home run champ.

Dave Kingman holds the Mets career record for home run frequency—he hit one every 15.1 at-bats. As a San Francisco Giants rookie in 1971, he Kong'd a Jerry Koosman pitch completely out of Shea—where it broke a window on the Giants' team bus.

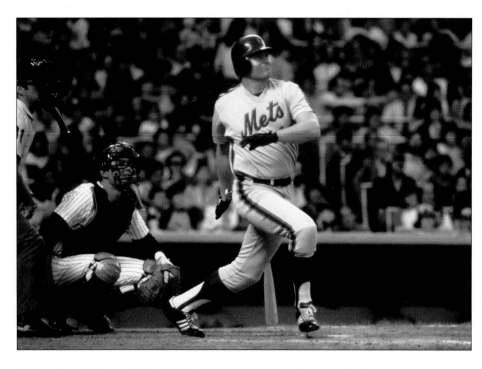

A Not-So-Super Star

At his introductory press conference in 1982, George Foster referenced Shea Stadium's proximity to LaGuardia Airport by boasting, "I'd like to warn the airplanes not to fly too low." It wouldn't be long before the team wished one was low enough for him to hop aboard.

At the time, Foster (a.k.a. "The Destroyer") was the biggest name the team had ever procured, and shortly after trading for him, the Mets made him the game's highest-paid player at $2 million per season. Foster hit 52 home runs in 1977 for the Reds, but his total in his first season in New York was exactly 25 percent of that. Worse, many felt that 25 percent was approximately the amount of effort the left fielder was giving the club. The helium-voiced Alabaman admitted to a teammate that he didn't dive for balls so not to risk injury, and he once drew the wrath of players and fans alike when his was the only butt left on the bench during a brawl.

Fans booed him pitilessly, and after hitting his 300th home run in 1984, he fueled their scorn by refusing a curtain call. Two years later, within 24 hours of accusing the club of racism because he'd been benched, Foster was released. He'd topped 20 homers in three of his four-plus Mets seasons, but his .252 average, modest RBI totals, and general failure to live up to his immodest aerial admonition had relegated a potential Hall of Famer to the Mets Wall of Shame.

Seeing Red?

Initially, at least, the trade with Cincinnati for George Foster (whose price was three mediocrities) was far more palatable than the one the Mets had made with the Reds five years earlier. In return for Tom Seaver, the club acquired four serviceable players who, no matter what they did, had no chance of placating the aggrieved Mets faithful. Outfielder Steve Henderson batted .287 as a four-year starter, and second baseman Doug Flynn dazzled defensively for four-plus seasons. And although young outfielder Dan Norman never panned out, pitcher Pat Zachry made the All-Star team in 1978, his first full season as a Met, before injuries undermined his promise.

George Foster was listed in a 1981 book as one of the "100 Greatest Players of All Time." In 1982, he signed a big-money deal with the Mets, with whom he would become one of the greatest busts of all time.

JESSE OROSCO WORE THIS GLOVE AS A ROOKIE IN 1979. IN 24 MAJOR-LEAGUE SEASONS, HE WOULD BE CHARGED WITH ONLY FOUR ERRORS— THE SECOND-FEWEST EVER BY SOMEONE WHO PLAYED AT LEAST 1,000 GAMES.

WALLY BACKMAN'S UNIFORM WAS CUSTOMARILY AS MESSY AS HIS SIGNATURE. AN OVERACHIEVING BRAWLER WHO THRIVED ON NEW YORK CITY'S ENERGY FOR NINE SEASONS, HE WAS CRUSHED WHEN TRADED TO THE TWINS FOR THREE MINOR-LEAGUERS WHO NEVER PLAYED AN INNING FOR THE METS.

POST SPORTS
WEDNESDAY, APRIL 6, 1983   30 CENTS

Hedberg, Rangers flatten Flyers, 5-3 — DELANO: P. 58 —

Nets' Brown denies pursuing Kansas job — KERNAN: P. 57 —

Leave it to Seaver

Packed house watches Mets nip Carlton, 2-0

By BOB KLAPISCH

OPENING day at Shea Stadium made George Bamberger, Steve Carlton and the largest Day One crowd in 15 years this much wiser.

Tom Seaver can be a winning pitcher this year. The Mets still have Lefty in their back pockets, and — imagine — Flushing is the home of a first-place team today.

"Doesn't feel too bad to be undefeated," Hubie Brooks said after the Mets won their ninth straight opening-day game 2-0 yesterday over the Phils in front of a paid crowd of 48,682 (more than 31,000 were in the park). "I think I like it."

Tom Terrific just like new
— HECHT: P. 60 —

So must Bamberger, who looked like nothing less than a genius for two reasons. After Seaver left a scoreless game in the sixth because of recurring problems with his left thigh, Bambi stuck with sinkerballer Doug Sisk for the last three innings when he could've easily panicked and sent for Neil Allen.

And when it came time to beat Carlton — for the Mets it was their 32d victory against him — the winning hit was provided by utilityman Mike Howard, whom Bamberger decided to start in rightfield only a day before.

"Optimism? There was plenty in the locker-room. And, really, why not?

"It means a lot to me to win a game like this," said second baseman Brian Giles, part of the two double plays the Mets made. "We were at a dinner reception Monday night and I didn't even realize we had that streak going. I'm glad it's still alive."

For the record, nine straight opening-day wins ties the modern-day major league record — the St. Louis Browns did it between 1937-1945.

But No. 9 was significant because, besides all the pomp and circumstance of Seaver's return, it showed he doesn't have to throw at 95 mph to win. For six innings, Seaver's fastball came in at 87 mph, but the location of his curve, slider and change were the real reasons why he surrendered only three hits, one walk and struck out five before his departure. For a team that is

Continued on Page 60

Steve Carlton fires away en route to loss No. 32 versus the Amazins.
Post Photo by Bob Olen

Bullets shoot down Nets, 95-89 — Kernan: Page 57 —

JUST RELEASED!
U.S. GOV'T REPORT
CARLTON BOX — LESS THAN 0.5 MG. TAR, 0.05 MG. NICOTINE

Herald Gazette
U.S. GOV'T REPORT:
CARLTON IS LOWEST.
U.S. Government Laboratory tests confirm no cigarette lower in tar than Carlton.

CARLTON IS LOWEST.

Box: less than 0.01 mg. tar, 0.002 mg. nicotine.

Warning: The Surgeon General Has Determined That Cigarette Smoking Is Dangerous to Your Health.

Displaying the near-perfect form that has become his trademark, Tom Seaver rears back and fires fastball during Mets' 2-0 opening-day victory over Phils yesterday at Shea.
Post Photo by Bob Olen

Young on beautiful day at Shea: P. 60

TOM SEAVER'S TRIUMPHANT RETURN TO THE METS IN 1983 TEMPORARILY REJUVENATED A FLAGGING FRANCHISE. HE SHUT OUT THE PHILLIES ON THREE HITS OVER SIX INNINGS IN HIS APRIL 5 HOMECOMING, OUTPITCHING FELLOW FUTURE HALL OF FAMER STEVE CARLTON.

IN 1976, CRANE CHIPS DISTRIBUTED A SET OF 70 DISCS FEATURING BASEBALL STARS, INCLUDING THESE TWO METS. KINGMAN CLUBBED 37 HOMERS THAT YEAR; LOLICH WAS THE FOURTH STARTER ON A STAFF THAT COMPILED THE THIRD-LOWEST ERA (2.94) IN TEAM HISTORY.

THIS IS THE MOST RECENT OF THE FIVE *SPORTS ILLUSTRATED* COVERS ON WHICH TOM SEAVER HAS APPEARED. THE FIRST WAS AS THE MAGAZINE'S 1969 SPORTSMAN OF THE YEAR.

CRAIG SWAN AND COACH JOE PIGNATANO TEND TO THE ONLY FRUITFUL PART OF THE LATE '70S FRANCHISE—THE BULLPEN GARDEN.

IRONY PRACTICALLY SOAKED THROUGH THE PAGES OF THIS GEORGE FOSTER COMIC BOOK FROM 1982. THERE WASN'T ANYTHING FUNNY ABOUT HIS ANGUISHED STINT WITH THE METS, AND IT OFTEN SEEMED THE ONE-TIME HOME RUN CHAMP'S ONLY PURPOSE AND DREAM WAS TO GET OUT OF TOWN.

Fortunes Down, Prospects Up

One Banner Day afternoon, a couple of fans paraded an entry across the Shea Stadium outfield that read, "Should reincarnation exist, this bed sheet would like the opportunity to return merely as a bed sheet." The obtuse implication was that a tribute to the Mets was not worth the fabric it was written on. A look behind the scenes in the early '80s, however, revealed clues that the fabric of the organization was changing.

Four years into GM Frank Cashen's regime, the uptick in the victory column was a mere five games. Still, the 68-win snoozer that was 1983 had its silver linings. Veterans such as first baseman Keith Hernandez (a former NL MVP acquired in June), center fielder Mookie Wilson (who stole a total of 112 bases in 1982 and '83), and reliever Jesse Orosco (who led the team in both wins and saves) were approaching their peak years. What's more, the farm system was aflower with exciting youngsters such as second baseman Wally Backman, third baseman Kevin Mitchell, and pitchers Ron Darling and Roger McDowell. Plus, the team had two of the greatest prospects anyone had ever seen—and they weren't even daily shavers.

In 1980, a lanky outfielder from Los Angeles with the musical moniker Darryl Strawberry became the first draft pick Cashen ever made for the Mets. Three seasons later, at age 21, Strawberry was the team's starting right fielder; he won the Rookie of the Year Award in 1983 and pummeled pitchers to the tune of 26 home runs. Two Junes after he chose Strawberry, Cashen's first-round selection was fireballing Floridian Dwight Gooden. "Doc" spent all of '83 in A-ball, where his 19-4 record and 300 (!) strikeouts in 191 innings made him look far closer to major-league caliber than any 18-year-old most scouts could recall.

As '83 lumbered into the dogs days of summer, the Mets—a woeful 37–65 at the

Dwight Gooden was an unaffected and unhittable teen in 1984, when fans crammed the stadium to see a pitcher compared to Sandy Koufax by the only player who ever faced them both— Pete Rose.

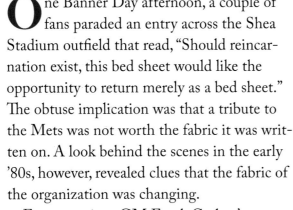

Veteran Phillies scout Hugh Alexander called Darryl Strawberry "the best prospect I've seen in the last 30 years." It cost the Mets $210,000 in 1980 to prevent him from accepting a basketball scholarship to Oklahoma.

This batch of players, including (from left) Jesse Orosco, Darryl Strawberry, and Keith Hernandez, would transform the down-and-out '83 squad to world champs. The arrival of Gary Carter and Dwight Gooden (and departure of George Foster) sealed the deal.

time—pulled off an unexpectedly inspired doubleheader sweep of the Pirates on July 31, with Orosco winning both 12-inning games and Bob Bailor and George Foster providing the walk-off ribbies. The team played .500 ball the rest of the way. It was something to build on, but there were still several black holes in Cashen's blueprint—the team was clearly substandard at shortstop and behind the plate, and the pitching staff was patchwork.

The greatest insufficiency of all, though, was that the ship was adrift without an anchor. Skipper George Bamberger (who, as a manager, made a terrific pitching coach) resigned in June. "Times are different," he opined. "The kids today, well, you can't yell

at them. When I was a kid, they yelled at me and I accepted it." The club's haplessness also turned Bambi's interim replacement, the usually serene Frank Howard, into a yeller. He, too, proved not to have the composition or cunning to optimize a team that, for all its apparent potential, had just completed a seventh straight year of getting its brains beat in.

It wouldn't be long, however, before Cashen addressed every one of the team's deficiencies.

On the last day of the 1983 season, the Mets pulled up their bedsheets as merely another last-place team. They would, unbeknownst to even them, wake up on Opening Day of 1984 recast as an unlikely pennant contender.

CHAPTER FOUR

A RETURN TO RELEVANCE

1984–1990

SEVEN YEARS OF famine preceded seven years of plenty for the Mets, whose sudden about-face in the second half of the '80s rivaled that of Lazarus in terms of improbability. The genesis of the turnaround was the hiring of Davey Johnson as manager. His clubs contended in all six of his full seasons, but 1986 was special—that year, the Mets returned to the Promised Land.

The 1984 season ticket brochure exhorted fans to "catch the rising stars." That promotional motto was more harmonic than such other clunky slogans as "Are You Ready? New Year, New Team, New Magic" (1999), "Excellence. Again and Again" (1989), and "There's No Power Shortage Here!" (1983).

Teammates Keith Hernandez, Darryl Strawberry, and Wally Backman lived the high life in the mid-'80s, playing able baseball on the field and raising Cain off of it.

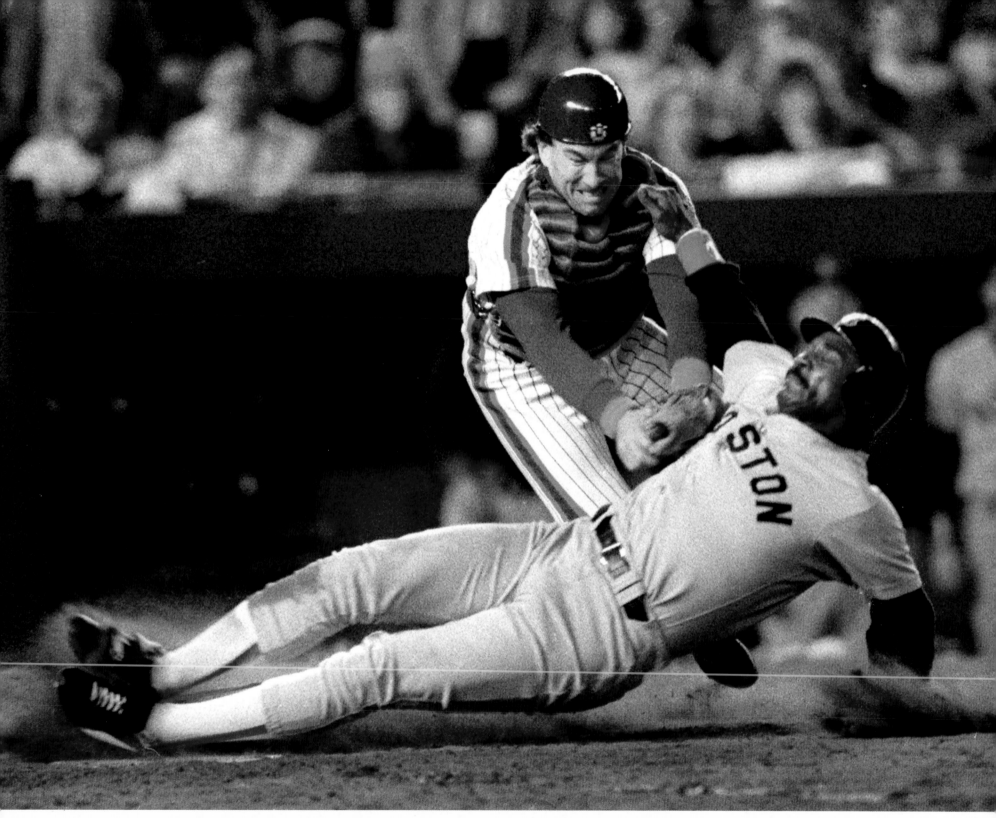

Left fielder Mookie Wilson gunned down Boston's Jim Rice at home in the seventh inning of Game 6 of the 1986 World Series. Three frames later, Wilson's innocuous bouncer would prove to be the definitive Mets moment of the last 40 years.

Davey Johnson

Davey Johnson entered Mets lore while playing for the Baltimore Orioles by making the final out of the 1969 World Series; fifteen years later, he was hired as their 11th—and ultimately most successful—manager. To a monochrome franchise lost in a black hole of defeatism and swathed in red ink, he was a Technicolor burst of confidence, innovation, and irreverence. "I guess I've got to teach them how to win," he quipped when he was hired after the 1983 season. And that he did.

The antacid-popping Johnson was a driven and diverse man. He earned a mathematics degree (which he gleefully plied as a pioneer in computer applications to baseball statistics), maintained expansive real estate interests, explored the air in his plane and the sea in his scuba gear, and even edited an investment newsletter; he also could be an old-school, foul-mouthed tabaccy-spitter who demanded heart from his players and would mortgage his soul to win a game.

The many facets of their new, genuinely fearless leader conspired to mold the Mets into World Series champs in 1986 and division titlists in '88; they also made Johnson the only National League manager ever to win at least 90 games in each of his first five seasons. But in his seventh season with the club, Johnson was fired by general manager Frank Cashen, whose authority he challenged relentlessly. "How about the good years?" Johnson inquired rhetorically after his dis-

Frank Cashen (left) described Davey Johnson—his pick to skipper the Mets in 1984—as "a rugged individualist." Wally Backman said Johnson had one rule: "Don't embarrass the ballclub or me."

missal. "The five seasons when we won more games than anybody? It made me look as though I failed completely."

His only deficiency was that the post-title Mets—a mélange of miscreants—failed to

realize dynastic expectations, a shortcoming that was perhaps enabled by their manager's boys-will-be-boys forbearance. What Johnson's critics failed to realize was that he made the Mets more than winners—he made them relevant again.

Cashen Crafts a Champion

When the Mets' new owners hired Frank Cashen to be the franchise's general manager in 1980, the bow-tied executive sloganeered fans with the motto, "The Magic Is Back." Not yet it wasn't, but it *was* Cashen's alchemy that conjured the Mets back into contention within five years and made them a champion in seven.

The former sportswriter had helped fashion the success of the Orioles teams that lost to New York in 1969 but won it all in '70. His approach was deliberate but purposeful; he favored building a team on the foundation of a strong farm system, yet he was unafraid to spackle the gaps by trading for veterans.

GM Frank Cashen pieced together the 1986 championship team with a combination of bold trades and slick player development, but he threw the franchise a curveball by disposing of several of the club's heroes by 1989.

Cashen brokered popular deals that bombed (George Foster) and unpopular ones that succeeded (Lee Mazzilli). He heisted stars in their primes (Keith Hernandez, Ray Knight, Gary Carter) and prospects in their nascencies (Ron Darling, Sid Fernandez, Howard Johnson, David Cone). He made providential draft picks (Lenny Dykstra, Randy Myers, Darryl Strawberry, Dwight Gooden) as well as imprudent ones (Terry Blocker, Stan Jefferson, Eddie Williams, Shawn Abner). He also screwed up royally by exposing Tom Seaver to the 1984 free-agent compensation draft. On balance, though, he was surgically brilliant, harmonizing patience with risk to craft what became, in 1986, a nearly perfect ballclub.

In the years following the championship, Cashen curiously and quickly dismantled what he'd so methodically assembled, usually to the team's detriment. By 1991, the Mets were again a sub-.500 team; Cashen stepped down after the season, his bag of tricks empty.

The Curious Case of Sidd Finch

The Mets reserved a locker for Sidd Finch at their St. Petersburg spring complex, but the phenom rented a room of his own across town, where he slept on the floor and ate only soup. Or so the story went.

In 1985, if any team were to discover a Tibetan yogi who could throw a baseball 168 miles per hour, it had to have been the Mets. According to a story that raconteur George Plimpton penned for *Sports Illustrated*, the club's crackerjack scouting department had spotted a French-horn playing orphan named Sidd (short for Siddhartha) Finch in Maine; the kid exploded soda bottles with his projectiles and claimed that, through some sort of mind control, "I have learned the art of the pitch." His quirks—he played ball wearing a necktie and only one shoe (actually, a hiker's boot)—could be addressed later. For days, the story set baseball abuzz; then someone discovered that the first letter of the words in the article's subhead—"He's a pitcher, part yogi and part recluse. Impressively liberated from our opulent lifestyle, Sidd's deciding about yoga—and his future in baseball"—spelled out "Happy April Fool's Day—ah fib."

Keith Hernandez

When the deal was struck in June 1983, it was difficult to see the trade that brought Keith Hernandez to the Mets as being part of some master plan. The team was going nowhere and things had been that way for a decade. The star first baseman was a batting champ and NL MVP while with St. Louis four years prior, but he wasn't hitting and, amidst tittle-tattle of drug involvement, was considered by many a long shot to survive New York City.

For all his dicey personal habits (chain-smoking, a special affection for beer, extremely late nights, and he later admitted, cocaine use), "Mex" was highly intelligent, magnetically charismatic, and a heck of a ballplayer. After his initial despondency over the trade, he came to the realization that the "team was about to explode. I wanted to be a part of it."

Indeed, Hernandez became an indispensable part of it. He swatted over .300 his first four seasons in New York and regularly verged on 100 RBI. As a first baseman, he was borderline revolutionary, not only providing stellar defense (he retired with a record 11 Gold Glove Awards) but also captaining the infield and communing with his pitchers to elevate the play of the entire team with his analytical tack to the game. In the clubhouse, Hernandez was simultaneously one of the boys and a respected veteran who helped keep his equally revelrous teammates focused on their mission. Mets broadcaster

Tim McCarver reflected that, "He brings an intensity and a presence to the club that just can't be replaced . . . . He makes everybody better around him."

Hernandez, one of the exalted heroes of the 1986 season, saw his career slowed to a halt by a series of injuries in his mid-30s. Today, he is an admired (if impious) Mets TV analyst and—of course—will forever be remembered as the man who befriended Jerry, dated Elaine, and was falsely accused of spitting on Kramer in an episode of *Seinfeld*.

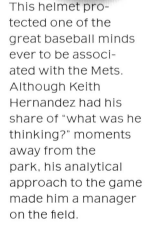

This helmet protected one of the great baseball minds ever to be associated with the Mets. Although Keith Hernandez had his share of "what was he thinking?" moments away from the park, his analytical approach to the game made him a manager on the field.

The Cult of Keith only grew when he appeared in an episode of *Seinfeld*, the plot of which revolved around the first baseman spitting on Newman and Kramer for razzing him after making an error. An error? Unlikely.

Ray Knight

In August 1984, the Mets found themselves, quite unexpectedly, in a pennant race. Sensing opportunity, Davey Johnson badgered a skeptical Frank Cashen into trading for third baseman Ray Knight—a two-time All-Star and pro's pro who Johnson hoped might mentor his young club through the pressure cooker. But for more than a year, the deal seemed inconsequential; the team faded down the stretch in '84 and Knight was virtually useless the next season because of injuries. Then came 1986, when Knight made his advocate look like a genius.

A hard-boiled competitor, "Mrs. Nancy Lopez" (as his teammates jokingly called Knight, the husband of the great golfer) was respected in every corner of the baseball industry. "Ray," praised Gary Carter, "is unmatched in character…a true giant." Whether he could still play through his pain was another matter, but Knight put the question to rest when he batted .298 with 76 RBI in 1986, delivering some of the most critical blows of the season. (One of those blows—to the jaw of Reds star Eric Davis, who had delivered a post-slide forearm shiver to the former Golden Gloves boxer during a July game—helped establish the Mets' reputation as obnoxious combatants.)

Knight was livid at Cashen for not attempting to re-sign him after he was named World Series MVP, and indeed, the team could have used his backbone the following years. He retired in '88 after a couple of unspectacular years in the American League, and soon put his expertise to work as manager of the Reds, then as an ESPN analyst.

On a team of trouble-makers, there was no dirt on clean-living Ray Knight, who played with passionate professionalism. In 1986, he batted .357 with runners in scoring position.

Broadcasters

Ralph Kiner, Bob Murphy, and Lindsey Nelson (left to right) were once the longest-tenured three-man broadcasting team in sports.

From the club's inception through 1978, its three voices on radio and TV were unchanged: Ralph Kiner, Bob Murphy, and Lindsey Nelson. Murphy continued on the radio through 2003, and Kiner still occasionally calls games today at 87.

Together they were formidable, but each articulated his own style. Nelson was often as loud as his sport coats, which ran the spectrum from plaid to paisley. Murphy was the artful pro whose flawless descriptions often made the camera seem superfluous. Kiner was the jock whose malaprops could fill a book but whose folksy style—whether doing play-by-play, color, or his now-46-year-old post-game show, *Kiner's Korner*—made him the "Hall of Famer next door."

IT WAS A MERE FORMALITY FOR FRANK CASHEN TO INVITE JESSE OROSCO TO SPRING TRAINING IN 1986, BUT THE GM WAS PRESCIENT TO CALL HIS CLUB "A DEFINITE CONTENDER." WITH AMPLE HELP FROM HIS KEY RELIEVER'S 2.33 ERA, 21 SAVES, AND CLASSIC POSTSEASON PERFORMANCE, THE METS WENT ALL THE WAY.

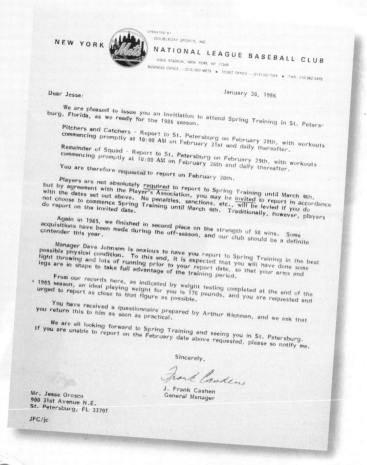

MET AND YANKEE GOOD FORTUNES CONVERGED FOR ONE OF THE FEW TIMES IN 1985. BOTH TEAMS NEARED 100 WINS, YET BOTH FINISHED SECOND IN THEIR DIVISIONS AND MISSED THE PLAYOFFS. FIVE MILLION FANS ATTENDED THEIR GAMES, WITH THE METS SLIGHTLY OUTDRAWING THEIR RIVAL.

FOR THOSE NOT VERSED IN BASEBALL HIEROGLYPHS, THOSE ARE STRAWBERRY SWIRLS ON THIS BASEBALL. STRAW'S CURRENT JOB AS AN ANALYST FOR SPORTSNET NEW YORK (SNY) AND A 2008 TOUR TO PROMOTE HIS BOOK HAVE KEPT HIM IN THE PUBLIC EYE.

NEW YORK
METS

RALPH KINER

BROADCASTER RALPH KINER, WHOSE AFFABILITY SHINES THROUGH ON THESE 1969 POSTCARD RENDERINGS, HAS BEEN IN CONTINUOUS SERVICE TO THE TEAM SINCE THE FIRST PITCH. HIS CALL OF "THAT BALL IS GONE, GOODBYE!" RINGS HEARTILY IN THE MINDS OF EVERY METS FAN.

I was at
Tom Seaver Day
July 24, 1988
SPORTS RADIO
1050 AM WFAN

ATTENDEES OF TOM SEAVER DAY AT SHEA WERE GIFTED WITH THIS BUMPER STICKER—AND A FLOOD OF MEMORIES. THE TERRIFIC ONE WAS FETED WITH A NUMBER RETIREMENT CEREMONY AND INDUCTION INTO THE METS HALL OF FAME.

BUBBLY GARY CARTER VOWED NOT TO MAKE THE LAST OUT OF THE 1986 WORLD SERIES, AND IT WAS HIS TWO-OUT, TENTH-INNING SINGLE THAT INSTIGATED THE THREE-RUN RALLY THAT OPENED THE DOOR TO A CHAMPIONSHIP. TWO MORE HITS FOLLOWED—AND BILL BUCKNER DID THE REST.

RACING ★ ★ ★ FINAL

DAILY NEWS
Sports

LUPICA SHOOTS FROM THE LIP
They 'Play Ball'
too late at night
Page 56

Sunday, October 26, 1986   Sports starts on Page 52

AMAZING!!!!
Mets' 3 in 10th forces 7th

It doesn't look like it from this picture, but Gary Carter and the Mets really bubbled over last night as they came from behind to beat the Red Sox, 6-5, with a three-run rally in the bottom of the 10th inning. That means Game 7 tonight . . . at Shea . . . winner take all.
Series coverage starts on Page 52

DAN FARRELL DAILY NEWS

"Kid" Carter

The press called him a savior. The players called him a prima donna. The fans called his name—"Ga-ry! Ga-ry! Ga-ry!"—over and over again. Gary Carter's first day in a Mets uniform has been called the most significant debut in franchise history, and after it was over, the future Hall of Fame catcher called it "the most joyous, most exciting day of my career."

"The Kid" was at the top of his considerable game when he arrived in a trade from Montreal with seven All-Star Games appearances and three Gold Gloves on his resume. The Expos, though, had wearied of his act.

When he dealt for Gary Carter in the winter of 1984, Frank Cashen said: "I figured we were one good ballplayer away from being a contender." He was correct.

His "act," peers mocked privately, was that "Camera Carter" and "Teeths" (as they derisively called him) was far more committed to photo ops than to them. But it wasn't an act at all; Carter was an authentically nice guy—always smiling and accommodating. He loved the game, played hard and hurt, had no discernable vices, and was unfailingly positive even though his back had more stab wounds than a typical night in the Bellevue ER.

If the Mets harbored any such reservations about their new teammate, it took them exactly one game to rearrange their priorities. On Opening Day 1985, at a frigid, sold-out Shea, Carter blasted a home run in the bottom of the tenth of a tie game against the Cardinals, securing both a victory and an indelible exclamation point in team lore. He ripped two more game-winning longballs during that homestand, establishing a pattern of clutch deliveries en route to back-to-back Silver Slugger-winning, 100-RBI campaigns.

One of the biggest hit songs of 1986 was Timbuk3's "The Future's So Bright, I Gotta Wear Shades." The title seemed to reflect both the long-term expectations of the Mets and the attitude of their optimistic catcher. Neither, however, would ever again exude the radiance they did in 1986.

This Gary Carter warmup jacket, autographed by the Hall of Famer on the right chest, was worn in 1986—the Mets' 25th anniversary season. Carter closed out the first quarter-century with what was then a Mets record for catchers of 105 RBI.

"Nothing Is Going to Stop Us"

With the 1984 hiring of Davey Johnson to administer a burgeoning array of talent, the Mets had become a spring-loaded franchise. The team that limped to a 68–94 mark in '83 spent most of July 1984 in first place before finishing with 90 wins (its most since 1969), six and a half games behind the Cubs. The Mets were even better in 1985—they battled the Cardinals in a furious NL East race that was unresolved until the season's penultimate day—but they ended up falling three games short of St. Louis despite posting a 98–64 record. As quickly as the Mets had descended into insignificance, they were again the toast of New York, and after their final game of 1985, the players frisbeed their caps into a sea of adulation at Shea. "I swore to myself, next year, by God, nothing is going to stop us," Johnson recounted.

If anything were to stop them, it would be the Cards, a squadron of jackrabbits who, via the histrionics of a taut pennant race,

Baseball was a contact sport for the '86 Mets. Ray Knight was safe following this collision, but Dodgers catcher Mike Scioscia would exact retribution two years later when his NLCS home run tied the series at two and eventually derailed New York's pennant prospects.

had become the Mets' most bitter rivals. The litmus test came just eleven games into the 1986 campaign: a four-game set at Busch Stadium. The opener, which the team agreed set the tenor for the rest of season, was unforgettable. His team trailing 4–2 with one out in the ninth, Howard Johnson hit a two-run homer, setting up a win in the tenth. New York completed the sweep, and the demoralized Redbirds went into a 1–9 spin from which they never recovered.

It was the beginning of a cakewalk; in fact, rarely in the annals of baseball has a team so thoroughly buried a league. The Mets' NL East lead did not dip below double digits after July 1, eventually settling at 21 and a half games over the Phillies.

On the way to 108 victories (no NL team had won more since 1909), they used their bottomless depth to dominate in all phases of play. The league's highest-scoring offense was kindled by different leaders in every key category: Darryl Strawberry's 27 homers, Gary Carter's 105 RBI, Keith Hernandez's .310 average, and Lenny Dykstra's 31 stolen bases. Six pitchers won at least ten games; two (Roger McDowell and Jesse Orosco) saved more than 20; and three of the five lowest ERAs in the league belonged to Mets' pitchers (Bobby Ojeda, Ron Darling, and Dwight Gooden).

The stuff of consumer frenzy and, eventually, mercilessly parody, Cabbage Patch Kids were issued for numerous teams in the 1980s. This Mets muppet came out in '86, at the height of the team's—and the dolls'—success.

The team's supremacy transcended the numbers, however. These Mets didn't just win—they intimidated. They blistered opponents with insults, and brawls were common. Rituals such as donning "rally caps" in key situations, taking curtain calls for every home run, and Carter's dugout dancing to scoreboard clips of The Three Stooges' "Curly Shuffle" chapped adversaries. Foe after foe took a beat-down on the field and left muttering about their vanquisher's lack of grace.

"Hey, they can hate us, they can resent us," scoffed the haughty Dykstra. "We got what we earned….We were the best. The good guys won."

Well, maybe not so "good." Off the field, the Mets were an unholy band of carousers that made St. Louis's Gashouse Gang of the '30s look like seminarians. Save a few straight arrows such as Carter, Mookie Wilson, and Ray Knight, the self-described "Scum Bunch" (think *Animal House* frat boys with unlimited funds) indulged with alcohol (and worse), trashed planes, slept minimally, and pushed every envelope of decorum. Such parochial misconduct seemed only to create a chemical bond that, within the ball club, nurtured a feeling of invincibility.

As the postseason loomed, Davey Johnson's prediction that nothing would stop his rampaging rowdies looked golden. Only two obstacles remained: an incommodious Astros squad, with whom the Mets battled mightily during the regular season, and an American League team in furious pursuit of its perceived destiny.

1986 Postseason

The Las Vegas oddsmakers had the Mets a heavy favorite to win it all in 1986. The odds against it unfolding the way it did were astronomical.

The NLCS opener confirmed that the pitching-rich Astros were capable of an upset. Houston's Mike Scott, once an ineffective Met, came armed with a somersaulting split-finger pitch that almost everyone was convinced was actually scuffed (doctored with sandpaper, which is illegal). He used it to fan 14 in a 1–0 defeat of Dwight Gooden.

New York was less mesmerized by Nolan Ryan in Game 2, winning 5–1. At Shea two nights later, a chess match ended with the Mets prevailing 6–5, thanks to the high drama of Lenny Dykstra's last-of-the-ninth two-run homer. Scott was back for Game 4, and he gave his opponents no chance

with a three-hitter. Gooden and Ryan were both dominant in Game 5 which snaked to the 12th inning before Gary Carter ended it, 2–1, with an RBI single up the middle. Game 6 was an epic struggle (see sidebar) that launched the Mets into the World Series against the Red Sox, who were chasing their first championship since 1918.

The initial game rung with familiarity: Boston won 1–0; Bruce Hurst edged Ron Darling, whose only blemish was an unearned run. A 9–3 thrashing by the Sox the next evening sent Shea fans home stunned. Revenge, however, was sweet for former Boston pitcher Bobby Ojeda in Game 3— Dykstra broke the ice with a leadoff homer and the left-hander did the rest as the Mets cruised to a 7–1 victory. New York evened things up the following night before reaching the precipice of elimination by bowing to Hurst again in Game 5.

Game 6 started with a skydiver, who brandished a "Let's Go Mets" banner, landing on the Shea Stadium infield in the first inning. After that, things got weird.

There is a sabermetric formula that evaluates a team's chances of winning at any point within a game. After the first two Mets batters flew out to start the bottom of the tenth

The legacies of both the 1986 Mets and Bill Buckner (above) were transformed the instant Mookie Wilson's grounder skittered through the wickets of the Red Sox first baseman.

This Lenny Dykstra swing generated a two-run homer that stunned the Astros, 6–5, in Game 3 of the NLCS. "The last time I hit a homer to win a game in the bottom of the ninth was in Strat-O-Matic, that game you play with dice," confessed "Nails."

The "Other" Game 6

As brash as the Mets were, they were not ashamed to admit that they did *not* want to see Mike Scott again in Game 7 of the 1986 NLCS, so a win in Game 6 against the far less intimidating Bob Knepper was mandatory. It took 16 innings and nearly five hours, but New York did manage to accomplish their mission.

Houston's first-inning three-spot was the extent of the scoring into the ninth, but then Lenny Dykstra's triple sparked a tying rally capped by Ray Knight's one-out, two-strike sacrifice fly. After Roger McDowell twirled five scoreless relief innings, each team tallied one run in the 14th. Two frames later, the Mets staged another three-run rally that was again catalyzed by Dykstra and Knight. It took Jesse Orosco 24 excruciating pitches to weather an Astros insurgence and lock down a 7–6 triumph—and a date in the World Series.

Ray Knight watches the Game 7 home run that gave the Mets a permanent lead. Knight earned World Series MVP honors with a .391 batting average and five RBI.

inning—which left the team one out away from a 5–3 loss—this measurement stood at 1 percent. It rose to four percent after Carter singled, then doubled when Kevin Mitchell did the same, and reached 19 percent after Ray Knight drove home a run. What happened next was immeasurable madness: A wild pitch tied the game at five, then Mookie Wilson hit a grounder that "bounced and bounced, and then it didn't bounce," according to first baseman Bill Buckner, under whose glove it trickled to give the Mets the most improbable victory in post-season history.

For the record, a brilliant long-relief effort by Sid Fernandez keyed the Mets'

8–5 clinch job two days hence, but the outcome of Game 7 seemed almost as anti-climactic as it did inevitable.

"Regardless of the jealousy, the envy, the hatred that exists for us, we have to be considered a great team now," pronounced Carter. Smart money said they'd be a great team for years to come.

Reliever Jesse Orosco, who was nearly perfect in the fall classic, saved Games 4 and 7. In his arms is Gary Carter, whose nine RBI accounted for nearly a third of the Mets' total runs.

Oh Doctor!

Having been burned by prized pitching prospect Tim Leary three years earlier, Frank Cashen was loath to expose his next can't-miss hurler, Dwight Gooden, to the rigors of the major leagues in 1984. The right-hander from Tampa was only 19, and he had never pitched above Class-A. Davey Johnson—beguiled by Gooden's crackling fastball, a curve (soon to be dubbed "Lord Charles") that turned legs to jelly, and poise beyond his years—had no such qualms. The manager prevailed, and for the next two years the kid was as unhittable as they come.

Gooden became "Dr. K" that season—baseball's youngest-ever All-Star, Rookie of the Year, and strikeout champion (with 276). He was even better in 1985, as he became the youngest-ever Cy Young Award winner thanks to a 24–4 record, a 1.53 ERA, and 268 punchouts.

It was around this time that Sandy Koufax declared, "I'd trade my past for his future." That, as it turned out, would have been a bad deal. Starting in 1987, Doc's dominant days became less frequent. He remained a winning pitcher through '91, but only occasionally did he vaporize hitters the way he once routinely did. Theories abounded: his release point was inconsistent, he overused his two-seam fastball, he was hurt, his confidence had evaporated, he altered his delivery, overcoaching confused him. The truth was more alarming.

Because everyone loved the good Doctor—because by nature he was affable, humble,

> "They shouldn't try to compare Dwight with Sandy Koufax or Nolan Ryan or anyone else because there is no comparison," Davey Johnson said of the young Gooden. "They should be comparing the others to Dwight."

The "Physician's" Assistants

Gooden had plenty of help in 1986. Bobby Ojeda, who had left the Red Sox acrimoniously the year before, was a lefty who featured a pitch that Gary Carter dubbed a "dead fish"—the best changeup he'd ever caught. Ojeda led his more illustrious rotation mates in wins (18) and ERA (2.57). Carter mischievously called Ron Darling (15–6, 2.81) "Mr. Perfect" not for his devastating splitter, but because the handsome and erudite Yaley's habits included blow-drying the warm-up sweat out of his hair before a start. Sid Fernandez (16–6) was a rotund and endearingly naïve Hawaiian who struck out 200 hitters. Rick Aguilera (10–7), who manned the fifth rotation slot, went on to become a great closer with the Twins.

The front four of the Mets rotation—Bobby Ojeda, Sid Fernandez, Ron Darling, and Dwight Gooden—were baseball's best. The average major league starter's ERA in 1986 was 4.06; theirs was 2.92.

and mannerly; because he had everything a franchise would want in its poster boy—it was unfathomable that he had developed a ruthless substance-abuse problem. During the '86 season, his behavior became uncharacteristic and unpredictable. The following spring training, he tested positive for cocaine, and for years afterward, there were hints that he never really stayed clean.

Co-owner Nelson Doubleday Jr. (left) is flanked by his most valuable asset, Doc Gooden, in 1984. By the time Doubleday divested his stake in the Mets in 2002, the pitcher was back in Tampa fruitlessly pursuing sobriety.

Gooden was released in 1994 after he violated the terms of his drug treatment program. Although he started his Mets career by winning 134 of his first 188 decisions, he lost 31 of his final 54. He knocked around with other clubs until 2000, and his personal life remained turbulent even after his retirement—he wound up incarcerated in '06 after a succession of addiction-related transgressions.

During the Mets' first homestand at Citi Field in 2009 (a season that also saw Gooden's nephew, Gary Sheffield, don the orange and blue), Doc got in trouble yet again—for inscribing his autograph on a wall at the request of a fan. "It's a brand new building... it wasn't meant to write all over the walls," complained the team's PR boss, who announced it would be painted over. However, a huge fan backlash compelled the club not only to preserve the signature behind plexiglass, but also solicit those of other franchise greats. Once again, there was a Doctor in the Mets' house.

METS MEMORABILIA

A METS VICTORY IN THE DECIDING CONTEST OF THE 1986 WORLD SERIES SEEMED A FORGONE CONCLUSION AFTER THE MIRACLE OF GAME 6, BUT IT WASN'T EASY. THEY TRAILED 3-0 INTO THE SIXTH INNING AND CAPTURED THE LEAD FOR GOOD WHEN SERIES MVP RAY KNIGHT (PICTURED BELOW) HOMERED TO LEAD OFF THE SEVENTH.

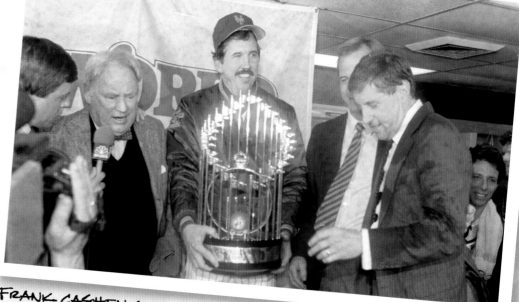

FRANK CASHEN AND DAVEY JOHNSON WERE THE BRAINS BEHIND THE CHAMPIONSHIP, BUT AFTERWARD WERE OF TWO DIFFERENT MINDS REGARDING TO HOW TO CULTIVATE IT INTO A DYNASTY.

DOC GOODEN WAS ALWAYS WILLING TO SIGN A BALL, OR ANYTHING ELSE. DESPITE HIS TRAVAILS, METS FANS HAVE NEVER ABANDONED THEIR MID-1980S HERO, WHO RECEIVED A THUNDEROUS OVATION AT THE SHEA STADIUM FAREWELL. IN 2009, HE WAS HIRED AS SENIOR V.P. OF THE INDEPENDENT NEWARK BEARS.

GIANTS RALLY PAST SKINS TO TIE FOR FIRST: GOLA/P. 88

POST SPORTS

Straw ignores Ray's peace plea — YOUNG: P. 91 —

Comeback kids follow the script — STEINBRENNER: P. 88 —

TUESDAY, OCTOBER 28, 1986 35 CENTS

WE'RE #1

Amazin's rally past Red Sox to win Series

By BOB KLAPISCH

THEY SPOKE thousands of words — but in reality they were speechless. The Mets were too numb to make sense. They chugged champagne. They hugged each other. They wept. They exchanged looks that said: The world is ours.

It took seven exhausting games, but the World Series ended last night at 11:26. It was the Mets who outlasted the Red Sox, 8-5. It was the Mets who scored eight runs in the final three innings — capturing their first World Championship since 1969. It is the Mets who can now shake their fists at the National League. Finally? Yes. Finally.

"Regardless of the jealousy, the envy, the hatred that exists for us, we have to be considered a great team now. We have to," Gary Carter said. "We showed our true character in this Series. This team is . . . I don't know. I really don't know what to say."

Carter — like every other champagne—

Continued on Page 90

Series MVP Ray Knight celebrates 7th-inning homer that gave Mets 4-3 lead last night at Shea.

JESSE OROSCO   DARRYL STRAWBERRY   LENNY DYKSTRA
BOB OJEDA   Keith Hernandez   RON DARLING
NEW YORK METS
WORLD CHAMPIONS   Ray Knight   Dave Johnson
◄ 1986 ►
Gary Carter   DWIGHT GOODEN

THIS BAT COMMEMORATES THE METS' 1986 CHAMPIONSHIP TEAM, THEIR SECOND. THEY'LL CATCH THOSE DAMN YANKEES IN NO TIME!

1986 WORLD SERIES

$40.00

Gate **B** Box **12** Row **H** Seat **2**

GAME 1

FIELD BOX

SHEA STADIUM

WORLD SERIES 1986™

VS.
AMERICAN LEAGUE CHAMPIONS

GAME 1

RAIN CHECK subject to the conditions set forth on back hereof.
COUPON
DO NOT DETACH THIS
PETER V. UEBERROTH
Commissioner of Baseball

HOMETOWN FANS WHO HELD THESE TICKETS HAD NOTHING TO CHEER ABOUT IN THE FIRST FOUR GAMES OF THE 1986 WORLD SERIES. THE VISITING TEAM WON EVERY ONE OF THEM.

THOUGH NOT EVEN THE SELLER OF THIS ITEM KNEW WHO TILLOTSON WAS, THIS 1986 WORLD SERIES RING SOLD FOR $7,000 IN 2009.

JESSE OROSCO WORE #47 IN HIS TIME WITH THE CLUB. THE NUMBER HAS ADDED SIGNIFICANCE SINCE IT ALSO BELONGED TO JAY HOOK, THE FIRST PITCHER EVER TO WIN A GAME FOR THE METS.

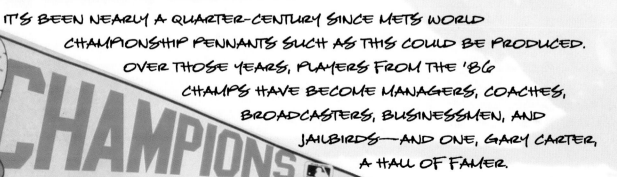

IT'S BEEN NEARLY A QUARTER-CENTURY SINCE METS WORLD CHAMPIONSHIP PENNANTS SUCH AS THIS COULD BE PRODUCED. OVER THOSE YEARS, PLAYERS FROM THE '86 CHAMPS HAVE BECOME MANAGERS, COACHES, BROADCASTERS, BUSINESSMEN, AND JAILBIRDS—AND ONE, GARY CARTER, A HALL OF FAMER.

Nails & Mookie

If the title of Timbuk3's smash described the cleanup-hitting Gary Carter, then it was the title of the 1986 Oscar-winning film *Platoon* that connoted the championship team's leadoff and center field positions.

Lenny Dykstra and Mookie Wilson had spots in the field and at the top of the batting order in common, but not much more. The lefty-hitting Dykstra was a wooly firecracker of a performer and an iconoclastic personality, a dirtbag with chew in his cheek. The switch-hitting Wilson (whom Davey Johnson preferred to use against southpaws) was a placid man and graceful player who was married in a ballpark and sang gospel songs. Whereas Mookie was a quiet leader, Dykstra (who called everyone "Dude" in his uninterpretable SoCal dialect) never shut up, his every move off the field leading only to trouble.

Dykstra literally and figuratively sped through the Mets system, once stealing 105 bases for his Class-A team. The fearless "Nails"—only 23 and in his first full season in '86—was a maniacal competitor and endless source of big hits and inspiring plays. The secret of his success, said Billy Beane—a former teammate who later became the protagonist of the bestseller *Moneyball* as the Oakland A's GM—was that he had "no concept of failure." Dykstra's Mets career was a failure only in its brevity: In 1989, he left New York to become a three-time All-Star for the Phillies.

The more stable Wilson spent a decade in New York; he later managed in the Mets system and served as a coach with the big club from 1997 to 2002. He is most renowned for slapping the thousand-hopper that Bill Buckner whiffed on in the 1986 World Series, but he ranks second in team history in stolen bases and is one of the club's seven 1,000-hit men.

Neither Dykstra nor Wilson was done justice individually by Johnson's platoon arrangement in the late '80s, but considering the team's success, things couldn't have been scripted any better.

Speedy Mookie Wilson held team records for stolen bases (281) and triples (62) until the even speedier Jose Reyes eclipsed both in 2008.

Lenny Dykstra's high-risk personality was as menacing as his high-impact ability. His first career ended in 1996 with a back injury; his second—in high finance—was derailed in 2009 by eight-digit debt and bankruptcy.

Darryl Strawberry

The triumphant, tragic story of Darryl Strawberry staggers with its complexity. Once he held the world in the palm of his hand; when he clenched his fist, however, the world retaliated with furious vengeance. A certain Hall of Fame career was terminated and so, almost, was his life.

The game always came easy to Straw. There were scouts who claimed never to have seen a more archetypal baseball machine. Strawberry was the 1983 NL Rookie of the Year and he made the All-Star team in all seven of his Mets seasons thereafter. His 252 home runs for the club remain a record.

Strawberry, however, seemed perpetually tormented. Though likable and generous when sober, he was more often surly, insensitive, and given to passionless play. Not even the 1986 world title gratified him. "I knew that my triumph would soon dissolve into loneliness and anger," he said. No matter his triumphs, Strawberry always invited an insinuation of underachievement. Keith Hernandez (once cold-cocked by the right fielder during a photo session) called him "the most frustrating man I have ever played with."

Developments during and since his career have helped to explain the recalcitrance. Straw's rap sheet includes drugs, alcohol, spousal abuse, tax evasion, a false report of theft, solicitation of prostitution, expulsion from a rehab center, weapons, familial entanglements, and violation of probation. Amidst it all, he received but squandered numerous opportunities with other teams.

Colon cancer and a lost kidney nearly robbed him of more chances at redemption, but Strawberry is currently making the best of his life as an evangelical Christian, the author of his cautionary tale, a philanthropist, and a studio analyst for Mets television. A few years back, he gave away his house, a Rolex, and his luxury cars to friends. "I got tired of it all," he rationalized. "I live a simple life now; I'm a simple man." And with that statement, Darryl Strawberry's story waxes even more complex.

Darryl Strawberry was often compared to Willie Mays (who is shown here presenting Strawberry the 1983 Rookie of the Year plaque) in terms of gifts and on-field grace. On their 30th birthdays, Straw had 280 home runs and 201 stolen bases; Mays had 285 and 207.

In the play *The Sweetest Swing in Baseball*—which is still popular on the theater circuit—the main character adopts the personality of Darryl Strawberry so she will appear schizophrenic. Art imitating life.

Jesse Orosco & Roger McDowell

Should opposing hitters somehow have managed to chase one of the Mets' brilliant starting pitchers in the mid-'80s, their troubles were far from over. New York's bullpen tandem of the era—Jesse Orosco and Roger McDowell—is recognized as one of the most lethal lefty-righty combos ever.

No one was thrilled to see Jerry Koosman dealt to the Minnesota Twins in 1978, especially since they'd never heard of Orosco, the 21-year-old "player to be named later" out of rookie ball whom the Mets got in return. As it turns out, GM Joe McDonald never made a better trade. Orosco, a slider-slinging southpaw, became the nucleus of the pen three years later. In '83, he finished third in NL Cy Young Award balloting and began a four-year period in which he won 39 games and saved 86 while compiling a 2.22 ERA. He made some of the most critical pitches of the 1986 postseason, claiming three wins in the NLCS and firing scoreless ball in the World Series while being on the mound for the final, exultant outs of both.

Orosco's stats were even more remarkable in the context of his tag-team with McDowell, whom Davey Johnson used just as confidently late in the game. The right-handed sinkerballer collected 32 victories and 80 saves from 1985 to '88, but he also left a treasured impression "off the books." If his teammates were baking soda, McDowell was the vinegar. The most relentless prankster in team history, he specialized in the "hot foot," but his creative capers included shagging fly balls naked before the Shea gates opened and wearing his pants on his head and his shoes on his hands during a nationally televised game.

Orosco would ultimately pitch in more games (1,252) than anyone else in the history of baseball. He retired after the 2003 season at the age of 46—he was, for several years, the last remaining '86 Met in the majors despite having been one of the older players on that team at 29. McDowell went on to become the pitching coach of the Atlanta Braves, a position he currently holds.

Roger McDowell was no-nonsense on the mound but all nonsense off of it. When hitters were slumping, he'd set off firecrackers in the bat rack to "wake up" their lumber.

Minutes before making his big-league debut in 1979, Jesse Orosco's stirrup caught on fire from a space heater in the dugout. He spent much of the next three decades extinguishing flames out of the bullpen.

HoJo

As one of the few teams with a surfeit of pitching, the Mets were comfortable dealing a prospect (Walt Terrell) to Detroit after the 1984 campaign. The object of Frank Cashen's affection was infielder Howard Johnson, a 24-year-old with latent thunder in his lumber and lightning in his legs. With Ray Knight seemingly ensconced at third base, the acquisition seemed redundant—but the payoff proved to be as substantial as that of any deal in Mets annals.

Except for the intermittent longball, HoJo's initial contributions were modest. But for a five-year period beginning in '87, he was a wellspring of home runs and stolen bases—in fact, he's one of only four players (with Bobby Bonds, Barry Bonds, and Alfonso Soriano) in the history of the game to ring up 30 of each in three different seasons. In '89 and '91, he was an All-Star and a Silver Slugger Award winner. Although those decorations came as a hot

Howard Johnson is the only switch-hitter ever to lead the NL in home runs (38) and RBI (117) in the same season. That was in 1991, after which he mysteriously stopped hitting from either side of the plate.

cornerman, Davey Johnson frequently abided HoJo's ungainly defense at shortstop just to get another big bat into the lineup.

The steady-as-she-goes HoJo avoided the extracurricular hullabaloo that surrounded his teammates, but controversy over the nature of his power stalked him. More than once, at the behest of dubious opponents, his bats were X-rayed for cork; nothing more than the pockmarks left by pummeling the most home runs ever by a National League switch-hitter (a distinction he's since relinquished) was ever discovered. He still ranks among the Mets' all-time top three in career home runs, RBI, and stolen bases.

Throughout the 2000s, Johnson imparted his offensive acumen as an instructor and manager throughout the Mets organization, and since 2007, he's been the major-league team's hitting coach. Few who have donned the blue and orange have served with more distinction.

METS MEMORABILIA

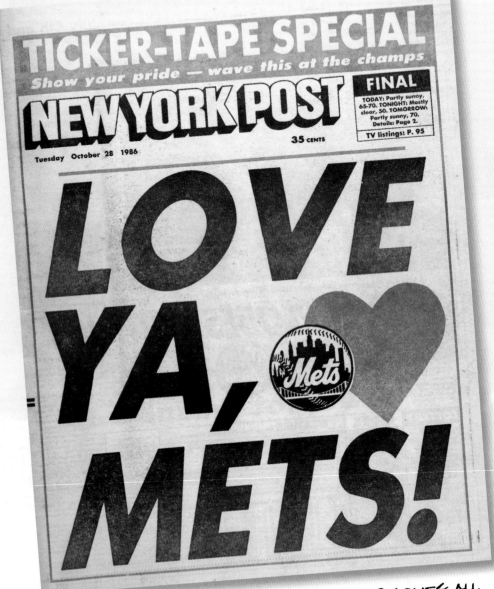

TICKER-TAPE SPECIAL
Show your pride — wave this at the champs

NEW YORK POST

35 CENTS

FINAL
TODAY: Partly sunny, 65-70. TONIGHT: Mostly clear, 50. TOMORROW: Partly sunny, 70. Details: Page 2.

TV listings: P. 95

Tuesday October 28 1986

LOVE YA, ♥ METS!

IN 2004, NEW YORK WAS ADORNED WITH PLAQUES ALL OVER THE CITY, COMMEMORATING FAMOUS TICKER-TAPE PARADES. THE 1986 METS WERE AMONGST THOSE HONORED; THEIR PLAQUES RESIDE ON BROADWAY, NEAR VESEY STREET.

RON DARLING CERTIFIED THIS MITT AS HIS "GAMER" IN 1986. A SHREWD ACQUISITION FROM TEXAS FOUR YEARS EARLIER, HE ALLOWED ONLY 22 EARNED RUNS IN HIS 15 REGULAR-SEASON WINS, THEN JUST THREE IN HIS TRIO OF WORLD SERIES STARTS.

DESPITE FIELDING THE HIGHEST SCORING TEAM IN THE NL IN 1987, THE METS' INJURY-CURSED PITCHING STAFF—AND SOME WOULD SAY TOO MUCH CELE-BRATING—PRECLUDED A REPEAT OF THE RAUCOUS SUCCESS OF '86.

NEW YORK METS

1986 WORLD CHAMPS

$1.25

SPECIAL World Champions EDITION

1987 OFFICIAL SCORE BOOK

BASEBALLS SIGNED BY THE 1986 METS TEAM ARE ADVERTISED FOR SALE AT OVER $1,000. FOR METS FANS WITH A SENSE OF HISTORY—AND RED SOX FANS WITH A SENSE OF HUMOR—THERE ARE EVEN BALLS ON THE MARKET AUTOGRAPHED BY MOOKIE WILSON AND BILL BUCKNER.

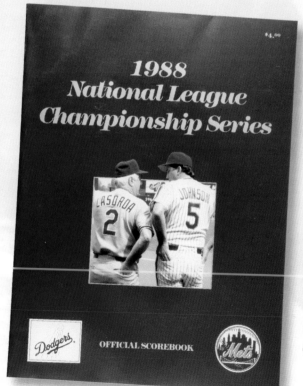

1988 National League Championship Series

LASORDA 2   JOHNSON 5

Dodgers.   OFFICIAL SCOREBOOK   Mets

$4.00

DYNASTIC DREAMS DIED HARD AT THE HANDS OF THE DODGERS IN THE 1988 NLCS WHEN THE METS, WHO WERE HEAVILY FAVORED, FELL TO OREL HERSHISER'S GAME 7 SHUTOUT. NO MET TEAM SINCE HAS WON 100 GAMES NOR HAD A LOWER ERA (2.91).

WORLD SERIES CHAMPIONS
NEW YORK METS
1986
LEE MAZZILLI

THE COMMISSIONER'S TROPHY IS PRESENTED ANNUALLY TO THE WORLD SERIES WINNER. THERE IS ONE GOLD-PLATED FLAG FOR EACH OF THE 26 TEAMS ON THIS AWARD FROM 1986, WHEN THE METS HAD A WINNING RECORD AGAINST TEN OF THE 11 THEY FACED.

David Cone

As with Howard Johnson three years earlier, Met scouts focused in early 1987 on a raw 23-year-old toiling for the Royals whom they believed had a higher ceiling than any pitcher on the New York roster save Dwight Gooden. For three bit players, the club acquired David Cone from Kansas City, and soon the Shea Stadium bleachers were packed with fans attired with the pointed "Conehead" caps popularized in the *Saturday Night Live* skits about surreptitious aliens.

The articulate but churlish Cone was more than a little wild both inside the lines and out. Iffy command of his pitches and impulses would sometimes erect a partition between "good" and "great" for him, but his effective wildness also made batters uncomfortable when facing his grade-A stuff. Hitters were most uncomfortable in '88 when he went 20–3 (the best winning percentage ever by a Mets starter) with a 2.22 ERA. Cone topped the majors in strikeouts each year from 1990 to '92 and fashioned a 19-K performance against the Phillies in 1991 that matched the NL record (since broken) for punchouts in a game.

Coney was shipped out the next year, by which time the Mets were getting reacquainted with futility. He helped Toronto to a title that season, then went back to the Royals to collect the 1994 AL Cy Young Award. After joining the Yankees' late-'90s juggernaut, Cone reinvented himself following a 1996 surgery for an aneurysm in his pitching shoulder. He did so valiantly, becoming the only pitcher ever to space his first and second 20-win seasons a decade apart by posting a 20–7 campaign in 1998. On July 18, 1999, he became the third-oldest hurler to spin a perfect game. Cone returned to the Mets for a last gasp in 2003. He retired with a World Series ring for every finger, but none that represented the franchise that made him a celebrity.

Kansas City owner Ewing Kauffman rued the deal that sent Cone to the Mets in 1987 as "the worst trade in Royals history." Cone passed on an opportunity to be a Mets broadcaster after he retired, but he later took the mic for the Yankees.

A Good Job Left Unfinished

Though regarded as featuring the deepest talent pool in the majors, something was missing from the Mets in the years that followed their triumph of 1986. Cashen systematically dismantled the tight-knit but high-maintenance roster, and many of the players who remained were undermined by injuries and/or personal problems. In '87, the team's pitchers alone spent nearly 500 days on the disabled list, but '88 started out looking like '86 redux. Until it didn't.

The regular season was a 100-win runaway that saw Darryl Strawberry lead the league in home runs (39) and new ace David Cone post the majors' best winning percentage (20–3, .870). Although the club entered the postseason without a key pitcher (Bobby Ojeda, who severed a fingertip with a hedge-clipper in September), the Dodgers—losers in ten of 11 regular-season confrontations with the Mets—were not expected to provide much resistance in the NLCS. Indeed, Met magic was back in the opener, when Gary Carter's double capped off a stirring three-run ninth-inning rally.

The Dodgers took Game 2 thanks to an uncharacteristically poor performance by Cone (2 IP, 5 ER), but Strawberry's three RBI led the Mets to a Game 3 win. Longballs from light-hitting catcher Mike Scioscia and the ever-heroic Kirk Gibson helped Los Angeles even the series with a 12-inning Game 4 win; the contest ended at 1 A.M. on a frigid Flushing Meadows morning. L.A. prevailed again in the fifth game while the Mets took the sixth behind a redemptive outing by Cone, but Game 7 was a 6–0 Dodgers romp that Keith Hernandez called the most disappointing outcome of his baseball life. Many New York fans still second that emotion.

Their dreams of a dynasty dashed, the Mets settled for being NL Eastern Division bridesmaids the next two years. Seven weeks into 1990, Davey Johnson was fired after his club left the gate 20–22. Strawberry, the last player in the starting lineup common to that of '86, left the team after the season. The final page of an era that featured many of the franchise's best teams had been turned. Soon, the Mets would be known as "the worst team money could buy."

"When you're going good it doesn't get any better than being in New York, but when you're going bad, it doesn't get any worse," Davey Johnson observed after he was fired.

Dwight Gooden was inconsolable after allowing a game-tying homer to Dodgers catcher Mike Scioscia in the ninth inning of Game 4 of the 1988 NLCS. Some say that the franchise lost its mojo at that very moment and has never really gotten it back.

CHAPTER FIVE

FROM THE OUTHOUSE TO THE SUBWAY

1991–2000

Being No. 2 was never good enough for Bobby Valentine. He is, however, the second-winningest manager in club history and led teams that were second-best in the division three times, second-best in the NL in 1999, and second-best in baseball in 2000.

FROM 1991 TO '96, the Mets endured six straight losing seasons thanks to haphazard trades and ill-advised free-agent signings that destabilized the team. Shortly thereafter, though, manager Bobby Valentine and general manager Steve Phillips detoxed the club's poisonous culture and sent the roller-coaster back up the hill. The prize at its zenith was a Subway Series against the Yankees that reestablished New York City as the epicenter of the baseball universe.

Kenner produced its Starting Lineup action figures from 1988 to 2001. This one of Bobby Bonilla was released in '92 amidst high hopes that the big-money free agent would revitalize production and attendance. Alas, the Mets' record in the "Bobby Bo" era was a dismal 218–302.

In 2000, Robin Ventura took then-Yankee/future Met Orlando Hernandez out of Shea Stadium in Game 3 of the historic "Subway Series." His roundtripper came in the only World Series game the Mets have won in the past 23 years.

Bobby "V"—For Victory

For a time, one couldn't tell Mets managers without a scorecard—there were six of them in the first seven seasons of the 1990s. Bud Harrelson was undone by his gossamer skin and distrust of the media, and the players felt no affinity for the button-down, push-button approach of Jeff Torborg, nor the negative, in-your-face tack of Dallas Green. But late in the 1996 season, Bobby Valentine—who previously had been a successful skipper with the Texas Rangers and in Japan—was summoned from the Triple-A club to take command.

Brassy Bobby V is a love-'im-or-hate-'im kind of guy. They still love him in Japan, where his managerial success has made him a rock star. A street, a beer, and a brand of bubble gum have been named after him.

Both as a man and a baseball man, Valentine was steely-sharp. Described as a "Type A-plus" personality by his wife, the former Mets second baseman was known for his total command of the game's nuances, aptitude for judging talent, and dogmatic dedication to his own way of doing things. Like Davey Johnson before him, Valentine was edgy, smart, and unafraid to challenge the status quo. (Valentine's outrageous stunt of sneaking back into the dugout after being ejected—wearing sunglasses and a mustache that was painted on with eye black—is a classic Mets moment.)

"He made everyone believe that everyone was important on this team," affirmed infielder Carlos Baerga. But no one player was as important to the Mets' about-face than "Bobby V." A roster adrift finally found its anchor.

Although the Atlanta Braves won the NL East by obscene margins every year in the late '90s, Valentine steered his 1998 team to within one game of a wild-card berth. That winter, the willingness of the front office to splay the coffers wide open to re-sign the club's stars (catcher Mike Piazza and pitcher Al Leiter) and add premium free agents (outfielder Rickey Henderson, third baseman Robin Ventura, and pitcher Orel Hershiser) sustained the positive vibe.

Even the rubber fish that hung on Bobby Valentine's office wall sang with conviction, "Don't worry, be happy."

Cashing Out

Three years after being a glitzy free-agent signing, Vince Coleman—who'd won six straight NL stolen base titles in St. Louis—was termed "a total mistake by this organization" by owner Fred Wilpon.

Thanks to the title of a book about the team by Bob Klapisch and John Harper, the free-spending Mets of the early 1990s became known as "The Worst Team Money Could Buy." Here's why:

- While with the Cardinals, Vince Coleman once stole 57 straight bases against the Mets without being thrown out; after the Mets signed him to a $12 million contract prior to the 1991 season, he stole nothing but their cash. The outfielder missed more than half of the Mets' games during his three-year stint with the team, cursed out a coach, shoved his manager, was investigated for rape, and injured three people when he lobbed a lit firecracker into a crowd of autograph-seekers at Dodger Stadium.

- The Mets traded Rick Aguilera (who saved 311 games after leaving New York) and Kevin Tapani (who would go on to win 143 games in a 13-year big-league career) and spent over $5 million for two-plus years of Frank Viola. "Sweet Music" was hardly bad as a Met—in fact, he finished third in NL Cy Young Award balloting in 1990—but the investment was questionable, especially considering that the comparatively affordable Aguilera (42 saves) and Tapani (16–9, 2.99 ERA) led the Twins to a World Series title in 1991.

- Outfielder/third baseman Bobby Bonilla signed with the Mets prior to the 1992 season for a record $29 million. His production was (at best) pretty good, but certainly not good enough to justify his salary or apparent selfishness. The boos for "Bobby Bo" at Shea swelled so loudly that he took to wearing earplugs.

- For $7.5 million, the Mets got future Hall of Fame first baseman Eddie Murray for the 1992 and '93 seasons. But despite his solid production, he polarized the locker room with his dour attitude.

- Bret Saberhagen won all of 29 games in four years for his $16 million, drawing his biggest headlines for assaulting reporters first with a firecracker, then bleach.

- A 7–15 ledger was all the team could squeeze from Frank Tanana for his 1993 salary of $1.5 million.

- Pete Harnisch "earned" $1 million per win from the Mets from 1995 to '97. His tenure with the team ended shortly after he disclosed that he was being treated for clinical depression, which was brought on by withdrawal from smokeless tobacco.

- Carlos Baerga's price tag for two seasons of mediocre play was nearly $10 million, not to mention the future of the guy they traded to get him: Jeff Kent, who went on to forge what may be a Hall of Fame career.

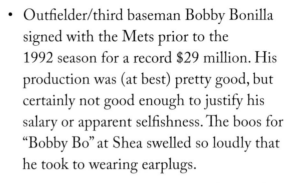

GM Steve Phillips, who has a degree in psychology, catered to the psyche of the New York fan when he brought in glamorous stars Mike Piazza, Robin Ventura, and Al Leiter, who would become the foundation of the 2000 NL champs.

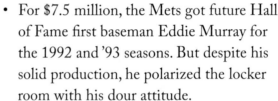

Left: Bronx-born Bobby Bonilla seemed to have the pedigree, the charisma, and the stats to own the city, but the worm in the Big Apple turned when the *Daily News* ran a supersized cartoon of the thin-skinned switch-hitter wearing diapers.

METS MEMORABILIA

THE TAGLINE TO THIS 1995 *SPORTS ILLUSTRATED* COVER STORY SAID IT ALL: RECKLESS YEARS IN THE FAST LANE, FUELED BY ALCOHOL AND COCAINE, COST FORMER NEW YORK MET PHENOMS DARRYL STRAWBERRY AND DWIGHT GOODEN THE PRIME YEARS OF THEIR CAREERS.

THIS DISPLAY DECLARED THE METS "ARMED AND READY" FOR 1990. FRANK VIOLA, DWIGHT GOODEN, AND DAVID CONE (PICTURED HERE)—WHO COMBINED FOR 53 OF THE STARTERS' 73 WINS—WERE READY INDEED, BUT RON DARLING AND SID FERNANDEZ HAD THE WORST SEASONS OF THEIR METS CAREERS.

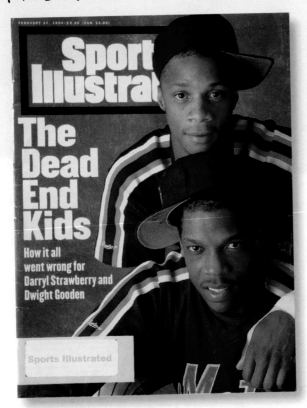

GREGG JEFFERIES TRADING CARDS AND OTHER MEMORABILIA, SUCH AS THIS STARTING LINEUP FIGURE, WERE SIZZLING HOT WITH HOBBYISTS IN THE LATE 1980S. THESE DAYS JEFFERIES IS CITED AS AN EXAMPLE OF THE PERIL OF SUCH INVESTMENTS: THE VALUE OF HIS MATERIAL PLUMMETED WHEN HE FAILED TO MEET THE HYPE.

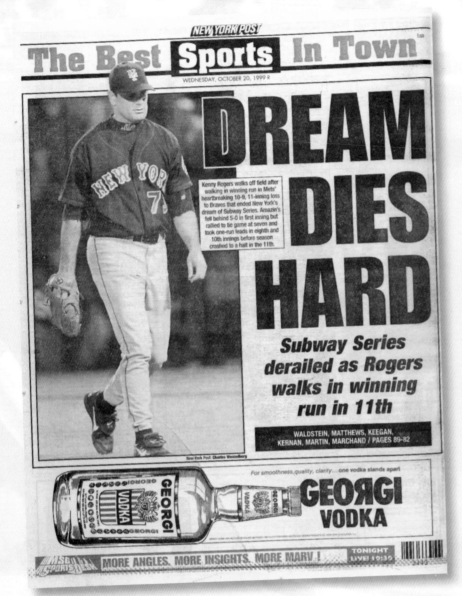

MAJOR LEAGUE BASEBALL INSTITUTED INTERLEAGUE PLAY IN 1997, AND THIS GAME PROGRAM COMMEMORATED THE METS' FIRST SERIES AGAINST AN AMERICAN LEAGUE SQUAD. THEY WON ONLY THE MIDDLE MEETING OF A THREE-GAME SET WITH THE RED SOX.

THIS BUMPER STICKER WAS ISSUED IN THE 1990S, BUT IN THE SUMMER OF '86 A PREPOSTEROUSLY CORNY BUT QUINTESSENTIALLY '80S "LET'S GO METS" SONG AND VIDEO (FEATURING METS PLAYERS AND A JOE PISCOPO CAMEO) WERE PRODUCED. "WE'VE GOT THE TEAMWORK TO MAKE THE DREAM WORK..." LA LA LA.

THE SEE-SAW SHOWDOWN IN THE DECISIVE 1999 NLCS GAME ENDED WHEN KENNY ROGERS WALKED THE BRAVES' ANDRUW JONES WITH THE BASES JUICED.

FORTY-NINE DIFFERENT PLAYERS SUITED UP FOR THE METS IN 1998, BUT IT IS TWO HALL OF FAME HOPEFULS FROM THAT ROSTER WHO ENHANCED THE APPEAL OF A BALL SIGNED BY THAT TEAM— MIKE PIAZZA AND JOHN FRANCO.

When Stats Aren't Enough

Perhaps unfairly, Kevin McReynolds is seen as a Mets antihero. The price to acquire him from the Padres in 1986 was five players, including Kevin Mitchell, who would win the NL MVP Award in 1989; the consequence of dealing McReynolds to the Royals five years later was the perceived necessity of signing Vince Coleman—one of the most notorious Mets ever—as his replacement.

There was no ignominy in K-Mac's stats. He averaged 24 homers and 87 RBI a year for the club and, in 1988, went 21-for-21 in stolen bases while leading the league in outfield assists. Instead, his disconnect with the rank-and-file was rooted in unrealistic expectations ("I can't tell you in all my years of scouting if I ever saw a player with tools like that," chirped GM Joe McIlvaine) and his supposed lack of

Kevin McReynolds was on the cover of the premiere issue of *Baseball America* and had "Hall of Fame tools," according to GM Joe McIlvaine. Only Howard Johnson drove in more runs for the Mets from 1987 to '91, but nothing McReynolds did could validate the hype.

A Savior Unredeemed

Accompanying McReynolds in the 1991 trade to Kansas City was the similarly overhyped—and similarly maligned—Gregg Jefferies. In 1988, at age 20, the sweet-swinging switch-hitter came up for one blockbuster month (he actually finished sixth in that year's NL Rookie of the Year Award balloting despite appearing in only 29 games), prompting the front office to anoint him a golden boy. *Sports Illustrated* even featured his peculiar training regimen, which included swinging underwater and shouting out numbers that were written on tennis balls fired at him for batting practice.

Jefferies, however, quickly became the most reviled man in the Mets' clubhouse. He proved narcissistic and uncoachable, as well as an object of jealousy among entrenched veterans (Roger McDowell once sawed all his bats in half). After three joyless, so-so seasons as New York's starting second baseman, Jefferies was traded; he ultimately made two All-Star teams as a first baseman with the Cardinals.

Gregg Jefferies hit .321 the last five weeks of 1988, but veterans were irritated when he was given Wally Backman's job the next year.

a competitive pulse.

So miscast was the laconic left fielder from Arkansas in the manic metropolis that he once carped of its fans, "It's almost like people are miserable, and they want to bring you down to their level."

In a twist of irony, McReynolds was brought back to New York in a 1994 trade. For Vince Coleman.

Whoa! It's the Fonz

Rich Donnelly, a big-league coach for more than a quarter-century, said in 2000 that Edgardo Alfonzo was "probably the most respected player in the game...the type of guy who honors baseball through the way he plays." Although "Fonzie" never led the team in terms of talent, he wrung everything that he could out of what he had.

No more pretentious than the Bart Simpson doll and red Christmas ball that dangled from his locker (to make it "look nicer"), the chunky Venezuelan dutifully played both second and third from 1995 to 2002. He made one All-Star team and won a Silver Slugger, but the essence of Alfonzo's game was that he was, according to Bobby Valentine, "spectacularly consistent."

Alfonzo's two best seasons coincided with Mets postseason appearances. In 1999, he

Hip Hip Hoo-REY

Rey Ordonez, who was the second ballplayer ever to defect from Cuba, exhibited a greater mastery of shortstop than any other Met to play the position. Bobby Valentine deemed Ordonez's glove "revolutionary" for the manner in which he backhanded grounders hit directly at him and for his dexterity in fielding balls on his knees and popping up to gun down his quarries. The manager compared Ordonez's ability to compute the trajectories of fly balls to that of Willie Mays; keystone partner Carlos Baerga saluted him as having "the quickest hands I've ever seen. I have to keep my eyes open, or he might hit me in the mouth with the throw." Ordonez won Gold Gloves in 1997, '98, and '99, and set a major-league record for shortstops with 101 consecutive errorless games in 1999 and '00.

hit .304 with 27 home runs and 108 RBI; the next season, he upped his average to .324 and notched 25 homers and 94 RBI. He also established a team-record 13-game playoff hitting streak during the Mets '99 and '00 postseason runs. In '99, he made only five errors at second base; none of them were on ground balls.

By the time Alfonzo left New York via free agency in 2002, he was prematurely on the downside of his career at 28. He played for the Mets' Triple-A team in 2006, but he was not able to complete his comeback with a return to the majors.

In 1999 and 2000, Edgardo Alfonzo was the only second baseman in baseball with 350 hits, 50 home runs, 200 RBI, and 200 runs scored. He also drove in 17 runs in 24 postseason games during that time.

One and Done

Four losses away from the most in the league, with four unlikely stars—the forlorn 1996 Mets were an anomaly.

Left fielder Bernard Gilkey hit 30 home runs, set one team record with 44 doubles, and tied another with 117 RBI. Center fielder Lance Johnson stole 50 bases and obliterated the franchise marks for hits (227) and triples (21). Todd Hundley's 41 roundtrippers were the most by a catcher in the history of baseball. Mark Clark's 14 wins and 3.43 ERA stamped him as an out-of-the-blue ace. But whatever superhero elixir this quartet ingested apparently was unavailable to its teammates or, after 1996, again to them. Gilkey was clunked on the head by a fly ball while gawking at an alien spacecraft in the '97 film *Men in Black*, after which he never again secured a steady job in the majors. Johnson and Clark were dealt to the woebegone Cubs in 1997 and were both out of baseball midway through the 2000 season. Hundley's production tailed off dramatically amidst rumors of performance-enhancing drug use, culminating in a disastrous stint with the Cubs during which he posted an anemic .199 batting average in two seasons.

Here are some other Met one-year wonders:

- *OF Johnny Lewis*: In 1965, one of his 15 homers accounted for the only run of a game in which Cincinnati's Jim Maloney no-hit the Mets for 10 innings.

- *P Bobby Jones*: He was an All-Star during his 15-win season of 1997 before deteriorating into one of the most hittable pitchers in the game.

- *3B Robin Ventura*: Brilliant in 1999 (.301–32–120), he failed to crack .240 for the Mets in two subsequent seasons.

- *OF Roger Cedeno*: Cedeno's 66 stolen bases in 1999 were the most in the franchise's first 45 seasons; then he was traded to Houston for...

- *P Mike Hampton*: The lefty won 15 games in 2000 and was MVP of that year's NLCS. He parlayed this performance into a ridiculous eight-year, $121 million contract with the Rockies, over the course of which he won a grand total of 56 games and missed two full seasons—and large parts of two others—to injury.

- *P Pedro Martinez*: After his 15–8, 2.82 ERA ledger of 2005, the Mets got next-to-nothing for their $50 million-plus investment.

Todd Hundley didn't weigh much more than 150 pounds when he was drafted, but in 1996, he managed to hit more home runs (41) for the Mets than he cranked in his entire 473-game minor-league career (39).

After rapping 186 hits for the 1995 White Sox, Lance Johnson signed with the Mets and became the first player ever to lead both leagues in the category.

Just a Walk Away

Steve Phillips needed less than two years to round up the horses Bobby Valentine needed to put a fright into the long-dominant Braves. A number of key contributors to the 1999 campaign—Mike Piazza (who posted 40 home runs and a team-record 124 RBI that year), Robin Ventura, Rickey Henderson, Roger Cedeno, Al Leiter, and Armando Benitez—were products of the young general manager's wheeling, dealing, and uninhibited spending.

The season was a heavyweight bout in the NL East from the outset, with no more than six games separating New York and Atlanta until late September. A seven-game Mets

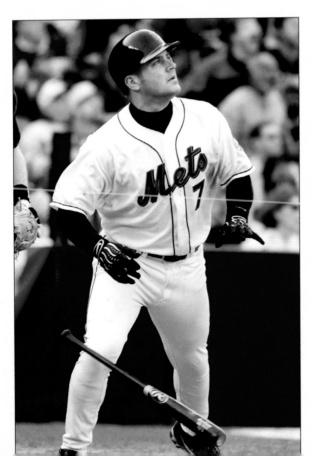

Todd Pratt was pictured on the box of the role-playing game *Ultima Online: Renaissance*. The little-used catcher proved to be a gamer during the 1999 NLDS, when he connected for one of the most important home runs in Mets history.

losing streak finally created some distance between the two clubs, and only four wins in the final week salvaged New York's opportunity to meet the Reds in a one-game playoff to decide the wild-card berth. Leiter's two-hit shutout earned the Mets an NLDS date with the Arizona Diamondbacks.

A backup catcher destined to be a footnote in Mets annals made himself an exclamation point as the hero of the Arizona series. Todd Pratt (a former pizza-parlor manager coaxed out of retirement for the 1997 season), batting in the bottom half of the tenth inning in Game 4, sent his team to the NLCS with a walk-off home run.

The first three games of the Championship Series against Atlanta were heart-tuggers: 4–2, 4–3, and 1–0 defeats. The Mets trailed 2–1 late in Game 4 and were in danger of being swept before John Olerud's two-run single in the bottom of the eighth saved them. It took Ventura's bizarre "grand slam single" (see page 114) to wheedle a win the next night. Game 6 was an exercise in breathlessness—the Mets scrambled back from a 5–0 deficit, assumed and relinquished leads in the eighth and tenth innings, then finally expired when Kenny Rogers walked home the clinching run in the 11th.

"I told them they played like champions," Valentine said afterward. "We don't have a trophy, but they did everything they had to." One October later, his feisty forces would get another historic chance.

METS MEMORABILIA

IN 1996, A SOUVENIR BANK CAME IN THE FORM OF A CHEVY PANEL TRUCK REPLICA—IRONIC, SINCE THIS WAS THE "WORST TEAM MONEY COULD BUY" ERA. FORTUNATELY, THE CLUB SAVED ITS PENNIES FOR STARS SUCH AS MIKE PIAZZA, ROBIN VENTURA, AND AL LEITER, WHO DELIVERED A PENNANT FOUR YEARS LATER.

THE YANKEES AND METS SQUARED OFF IN A REGULAR-SEASON SERIES PLAYED AT SHEA STADIUM IN 1998, AN EVENT COMMEMORATED BY THIS PIN. THE "BAD GUYS" WON THE FIRST TWO, BUT THE METS SALVAGED THE GET-AWAY GAME, 2-1, ON LUIS LOPEZ'S SACRIFICE FLY IN THE BOTTOM OF THE NINTH.

NO COLLECTION OF METS TEAM-SIGNED BASEBALLS WOULD BE COMPLETE WITHOUT THE ONE FROM 2000, THEIR MOST RECENT NL PENNANT-WINNING CLUB. SKIPPER BOBBY VALENTINE, WHOSE "JOHN HANCOCK" IS OFTEN ILLEGIBLE, IS VISIBLE HERE ON THE SWEET SPOT.

THE PROSPECT OF A SUBWAY SERIES GRIPPED NEW YORK LIKE FEW ATHLETIC EVENTS BEFORE OR SINCE. IN FACT, THE CITY DECORATED TRAINS TO REFLECT THE IMPENDING COLLISION—THE 7 LINE (TO SHEA) BASTED IN BLUE AND ORANGE, THE 4 LINE (TO YANKEE STADIUM) PAINTED WHITE AND BLUE.

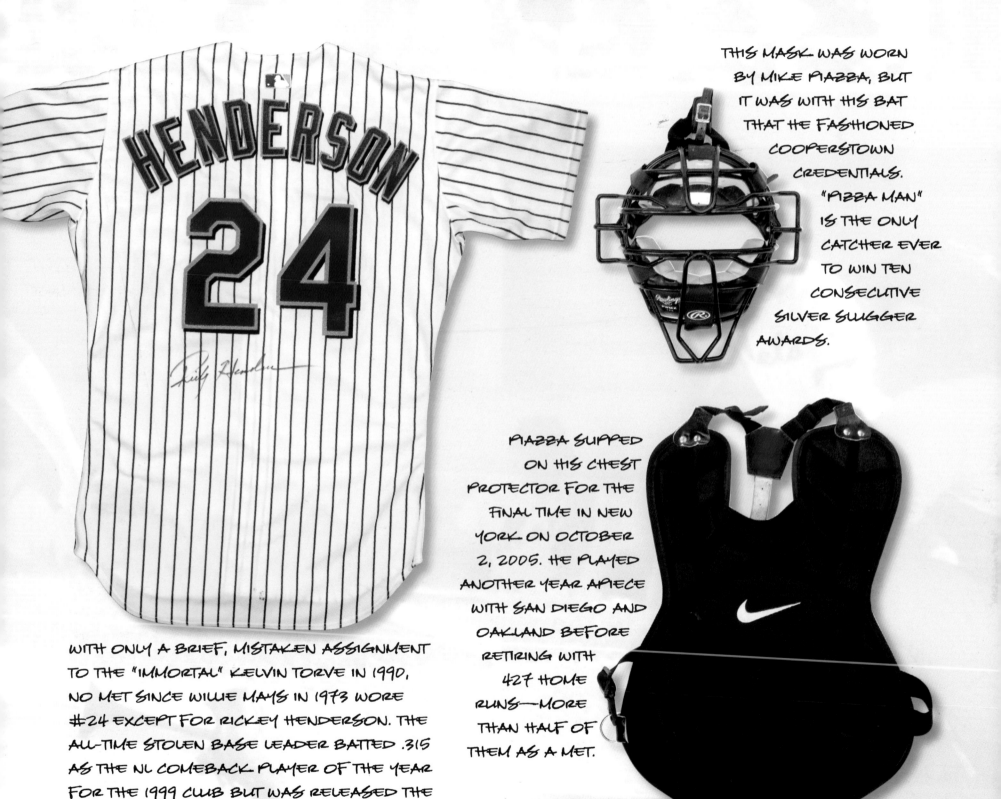

THIS MASK WAS WORN BY MIKE PIAZZA, BUT IT WAS WITH HIS BAT THAT HE FASHIONED COOPERSTOWN CREDENTIALS. "PIZZA MAN" IS THE ONLY CATCHER EVER TO WIN TEN CONSECUTIVE SILVER SLUGGER AWARDS.

PIAZZA SUPPED ON HIS CHEST PROTECTOR FOR THE FINAL TIME IN NEW YORK ON OCTOBER 2, 2005. HE PLAYED ANOTHER YEAR APIECE WITH SAN DIEGO AND OAKLAND BEFORE RETIRING WITH 427 HOME RUNS—MORE THAN HALF OF THEM AS A MET.

WITH ONLY A BRIEF, MISTAKEN ASSIGNMENT TO THE "IMMORTAL" KELVIN TORVE IN 1990, NO MET SINCE WILLIE MAYS IN 1973 WORE #24 EXCEPT FOR RICKEY HENDERSON. THE ALL-TIME STOLEN BASE LEADER BATTED .315 AS THE NL COMEBACK PLAYER OF THE YEAR FOR THE 1999 CLUB BUT WAS RELEASED THE FOLLOWING MAY.

Ain't It Grand? (No, Not Really)

One of the most peculiar plays in post-season history allowed the Mets to defer elimination from the 1999 NLCS for 48 hours. Game 5 was nearly six hours old and had gotten "to the point where your stomach was coming out of your guts," said outfielder Darryl Hamilton, when Robin Ventura singled—according to the box score—to drive in the winning run in the 15th inning. His "single" cleared the right-center-field wall. As Ventura trotted toward second base, a U-turning, euphoric Todd Pratt suddenly tackled him. Because Ventura never made it to the bag, he could be credited with only one base: a "grand slam single."

Todd Pratt's embrace of Robin Ventura didn't cost the Mets the game, but it did cost his third base-man the only walk-off grand slam in post-season history. One of baseball's other three "grand slam singles" came in 1976, when future Mets broad-caster Tim McCarver passed Garry Maddox on the bases.

Here are some other zany games from Mets history:

- July 22, 1986: Out of players because of post-brawl ejections, Davey Johnson rotated Jesse Orosco and Roger McDowell from the mound to left or right field—depending upon which Cincinnati batter was up—for five extra innings. Howard Johnson's three-run homer in the 14th ended the madness.

- July 4–5, 1985: Through 19 innings lasting over eight hours (thanks in part to rain delays), 43 players made 180 trips to the plate. Twice, the Braves extended the riveting agony in their ostensible final at-bat, including in the 18th, when Atlanta pitcher Rick Camp connected for the only home run of his ten-year career. At 4:01 A.M., when a 16–13 New York win was finally in the books, the Braves commenced their fifth of July fireworks show.

- September 11, 1974: The winning run of the longest game in team history—a 25-inning loss to the Cardinals—scored when pitcher Hank Webb's pickoff attempt to first was so wild that the runner, Bake McBride, was able to race all the way home.

- October 2, 1965: The Mets played the Phillies to a scoreless, 18-inning draw in a doubleheader nightcap; Philadelphia had shut out the Mets 6–0 in the opener.

You CAN Come Home Again

John Franco did not start any of the 1,119 contests in which he appeared, but for much of his 21-season career, there was no one better at the end of a game.

A tough, undersize kid from Brooklyn's Little Italy neighborhood, "Johnny" could have passed for an extra from *Saturday Night Fever*. He grew up idolizing Tug McGraw and fantasizing about rides in the golf cart that shuttled relief pitchers from the bullpen to the mound at Shea Stadium. After the 1989 season, the Cincinnati Reds—with whom he'd pitched for six seasons—returned him to his roots by trading him to the Mets for closer Randy Myers.

Franco's street-honed, "I got your back" personality and portside screwball-cum-changeup made him ideal for the role of ninth-inning enforcer despite his lack of exceptional velocity. Sometimes before taking the ball, he'd take a whiff of an ammonia capsule to whet his senses for the task at hand. "He'd kill you for a win," gauged Joe Russo, his old coach at St. John's—perhaps exaggerating only slightly.

For 14 seasons—a franchise record for a pitcher—Franco was a Mets assassin. He saved at least 28 games in half of those campaigns and led the National League in saves twice. His ERA in the 1990s was 2.81, lower than any other NL reliever with at least 450 games pitched. A team captain during his final years in New York, Franco pitched a final season with the Astros when he was 44 and holds the MLB record for most saves (424) by a left-hander.

On March 29, 2009, Johnny Franco took the mound to throw out the first pitch of the first game ever played at new Citi Field, a college tilt involving St. John's. He never felt more at home.

To honor his father, John Franco wore a New York City Department of Sanitation shirt under his jersey. He spent 14 seasons cleaning up other pitchers' messes for the Mets, saving more games from 1990 to '99 than any other National League pitcher.

Mike Piazza: The Last Shall Be Best

"You have to have a catcher," Casey Stengel reasoned, "because, if you don't, you're likely to have a lot of passed balls." And if you don't have a good one, he might have added, you're likely to lose a lot of games.

Steve Phillips realized this—as Frank Cashen had when he procured Gary Carter—and he engineered a deal to land Mike Piazza, the best backstop in the biz, in May 1998.

The two trades had much the same effect. Piazza averaged 39 homers and 118 RBI in 1999 and '00, and he powered the Mets into the postseason both years.

The son of a wealthy entrepreneur who was tight with legendary Dodgers manager Tommy Lasorda, Piazza was an anonymous junior college first baseman whom the Los Angeles skipper twisted arms to have the team select with its final pick in the 1988 draft. Astonishingly, Piazza was the NL Rookie of the Year five years later; he also won the first of his ten straight Silver Slugger Awards that season.

In 1998, the articulate Philadelphian became the center of the Mets' universe, the go-to guy for both Bobby Valentine (who called him "the best player I ever managed") and the insatiable New York media. At the pinnacle of his popularity, Piazza had to hire an assistant to open the 10,000 pieces of fan mail he received—per week.

In Game 2 of the 2000 World Series, Piazza was involved in one of the most memorable dust-ups in Mets lore. While

After this swing in 2004 produced Mike Piazza's 352nd homer as a catcher— a new record— previous standard-holder Carlton Fisk admitted, "when someone broke my home run mark, I was hoping it would be Mike. He carries himself with great class and dignity."

Mike Piazza donned his catcher's helmet in 827 games for the Mets. Only Jerry Grote has caught more games (1,176) or made more putouts at the position for the club.

fouling off an offering from Yankee hurler Roger Clemens—who'd knocked the backstop unconscious with a fastball in July—Piazza's bat shattered. A portion of the stick whirly-birded toward The Rocket, who retrieved the shard and flung it at Piazza, which led both teams' benches to clear.

After Piazza hung 'em up following the 2007 season, Lasorda recalled his "courtesy" draft choice's prediction: "When [Piazza] came up, he said this: 'If I stay healthy, I'm going to hit more home runs than any catcher in the history of baseball.'" And that's exactly what he did.

All Aboard!

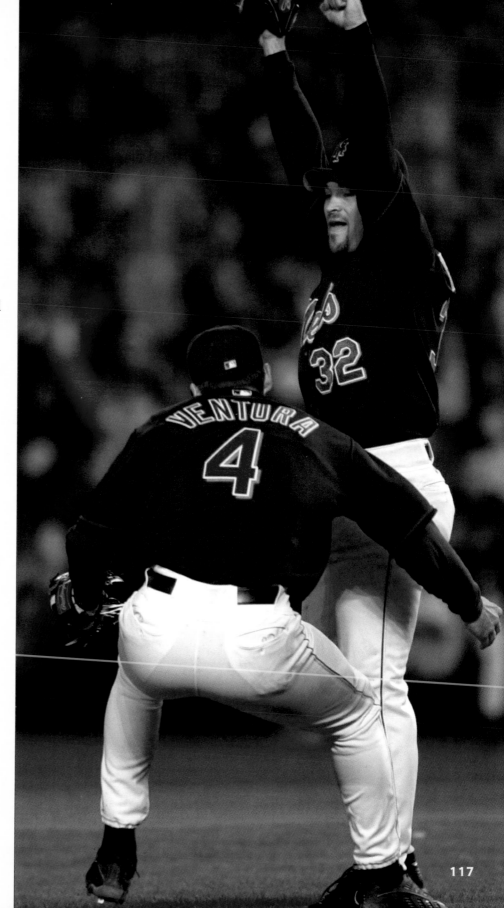

On October 18, 2000, three New York City newspapers ran identical front-page headlines. The World Series contestants were set: The Mets would face the Yankees in the first "Subway Series" since 1956. The "new" club in town had taken a roundabout route, but baseball in the Big Apple had finally come full circle.

The Mets' map to the postseason originated in Tokyo, where they split with the Cubs in the first two official games ever played outside North America. For all but a few days of the season afterward, the NL East standings bore their then-customary look: It was the Braves, then everybody else. The Mets made a couple of runs at Atlanta, but at the season's end, the Braves sat atop the division by a game. New York did, however, win the NL wild card by a wide margin, which earned them a date with San Francisco in the NLDS.

The series was a showcase for the unsung. Rookie outfielder Jay Payton resolved Game 2 with a 10th-inning RBI single; in Game 3, part-timer Benny Agbayani cranked a dramatic walk-off home run in the 13th; and Bobby Jones's one-hit shutout in Game 4 clinched the series. The subsequent five-game NLCS brush-off of St. Louis was all about Mike Hampton and his 16 scoreless innings in Games 1 and 5.

With 15 wins in 18 games, the Mets were peaking at the optimal time. The team

A commemorative hat was issued when the Mets and Cubs faced off in Tokyo to kick off the 2000 season. The two-game series was eerily tranquil because the typically boisterous Japanese fans had their noise-makers confiscated outside the stadium.

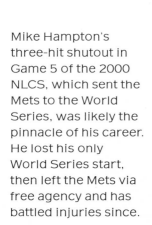

Mike Hampton's three-hit shutout in Game 5 of the 2000 NLCS, which sent the Mets to the World Series, was likely the pinnacle of his career. He lost his only World Series start, then left the Mets via free agency and has battled injuries since.

Mike Piazza was prepared for battle after Roger Clemens fired a piece of his broken bat toward him, but the Yankee pitcher won the war by allowing two hits over eight innings in Game 2 of the 2000 World Series. Not so in regular-season play, when Piazza hit .421 with four home runs in 19 career at-bats against "The Rocket."

The first all-New York World Series in 44 years was as contentious on the subways as it was on the field. More than six million fans, almost evenly split between the two teams, saw the Mets and Yankees play in 2000.

that had set a major-league record for fewest errors (68) in 1999 now favored force over finesse. Mike Piazza (.324–38–113) was the fulcrum, but six others contributed at least 15 home runs to the franchise-record total of 198 (since broken by the 2006 club that slugged 200 dingers). All five starters reached double-digit win totals (led by Al Leiter's 16), while Armando Benitez became the first Met to save 40 games. It was hard not to regard this assemblage as the fall classic favorite over a Yankees team that had posted only the fifth-best record in the AL.

From the onset, however, history seemed to seize the upper hand from momentum. The Yanks stole one-run decisions in Games 1 and 2 in the Bronx—the first on a 12th-inning RBI single by former Met Jose Vizcaino, and the second when a frantic five-run rally in the ninth fell one tally short. The teams traded victories at Shea before battling to a 2–2 tie into the ninth inning of Game 5. Then, Luis Sojo—like Vizcaino, a slap-hitting second sacker—singled home a run; another Yank scored on the play due to a throwing error by Payton. Piazza was potentially the tying run when he batted with two down in the bottom of the frame, but his threatening stroke to deep center was caught by Bernie Williams at precisely the stroke of midnight.

Mayor and Yankee fan-in-chief Rudy Giuliani professed a broadminded view of the proceedings. "This year's Subway Series introduced a new generation of baseball fans to all the excitement of having crosstown rivals meet on the field and play for bragging rights in the greatest city in the world," he reveled.

In less than a year, Giuliani would turn to baseball for respite from his city's greatest tragedy.

More Great Subway Moments

- **June 20, 1963:** The first Mets–Yankees Mayor's Trophy Game is staged; the Mets win, 6–2. The exhibition game is played annually until 1983, with the Yanks winning 10 of the 19 contests.

- **June 16, 1997:** Dave Mlicki of the Mets fires a 6–0 shutout as the teams do battle in their first-ever regular-season game.

- **July 8, 2000:** The rivals play a unique doubleheader, with the opener at Shea and the back end at Yankee Stadium. Behind Dwight Gooden and Roger Clemens, the Bronx Bombers sweep.

Yankee manager Joe Torre yelled "No!" as he watched a drive to center that, had it cleared the fence, would have tied Game 5 of the 2000 World Series. Moments later, it was Mike Piazza who hung his head while walking away from the enemy celebration after making the last, loud out.

MR. MET SAYS:

NO SMOKING

THIS NO-SMOKING SIGN FROM SHEA STADIUM IS ONE OF THE MOST ICONIC IMAGES IN METS HISTORY. THE BELOVED KEEPSAKE TYPICALLY SELLS ON AUCTION SITES FOR UP TO $800.

OCTOBER 4, 1999 – CINERGY FIELD, CINCINNATI, OHIO

NEW YORK METS (96-66)
LHP AL LEITER (12-12, 4.41)

Manager/Coaches	Pitchers	Infielders
02 Bobby Valentine	35 Rick Reed, RH	11 Shane Halter, SS
01 Mookie Wilson	38 Jeff Tam, RH	12 Shawon Dunston, SS
08 Cookie Rojas	45 John Franco, LH	13 Edgardo Alfonzo, 2B
20 Bruce Benedict	48 Glendon Rusch, LH	15 Matt Franco, 3B
52 David Wallace	49 Armando Benitez, RH	17 Luis Lopez, SS
53 Mickey Brantley	55 Orel Hershiser, RH	30 Jorge Toca, 1B
54 Al Jackson	73 Kenny Rogers, LH	33 Mike Kinkade, 3B
Pitchers	99 Turk Wendell, RH	Outfielders
21 Masato Yoshii, RH	Catchers	06 Melvin Mora
22 Al Leiter, LH	07 Todd Pratt	18 Darryl Hamilton
23 Pat Mahomes, RH	31 Mike Piazza	24 Rickey Henderson
26 Billy Taylor, RH	Infielders	25 Bobby Bonilla
28 Bobby Jones, RH	04 Robin Ventura, 3B	44 Jay Payton
29 Octavio Dotel, RH	05 John Olerud, 1B	50 Benny Agbayani
34 Chuck McElroy, LH	10 Rey Ordonez, SS	

NEW YORK METS	1	2	3	4	5	6	7	8	9	10	AB	R	H	RBI

TOTALS	R				
	H				

PITCHER	IP	H	R	ER	BB	SO

Each position on the playing field has a corresponding number used when scoring a baseball game. Here are a few symbols used while scoring:

1B:Single   BB:Walk
2B:Double   IBB:Int. Walk
3B:Triple   PO:Pole Off
HR:Home Run   PB:Passed Ball
E:Error   WP:Wild Pitch
HP:Hit By Pitch   SB:Stolen Base
DP:Double Play   LO:Line Out
SF:Sac Fly   FO:Fly Out
K:Strikeout   BK:Balk

IN 1999, NEW YORK SAT ATOP THE NL EAST AS LATE AS AUGUST 21, BUT A 13-15 SKID RESIGNED THEM TO THE NECESSITY OF A ONE-GAME PLAYOFF WITH THE REDS TO DETERMINE THE WILD-CARD ENTRY. AL LEITER'S SHUTOUT AND EDGARDO ALFONZO'S THREE RBI BOOSTED THE METS INTO THE NLDS.

A FAN COULD HAVE PURCHASED THIS TICKET—OR TURNED ON THE TV AT 5 A.M.—TO SEE THE METS PLAY THE CUBS AT THE TOKYO DOME TO OPEN THE 2000 SEASON. IN THE FIRST MLB GAMES EVER PLAYED OUTSIDE NORTH AMERICA, THE TEAMS SPLIT A TWO-GAME SERIES THANKS TO BENNY AGBAYANI'S 11TH-INNING GRAND SLAM IN THE FINALE.

THE 2000 SEASON-OPENING SERIES IN JAPAN WAS AGAINST THE CUBS, WHO STOOD IN FOR THE CARDINALS WHEN STAR MARK MCGWIRE REFUSED TO GO, CITING "GREED" BY MLB. THERE WAS MORE CONTROVERSY WHEN CHICAGO MANAGER DON BAYLOR REFUSED TO SHAKE BOBBY VALENTINE'S HAND PRIOR TO THE SECOND GAME BECAUSE THE MET SKIPPER HAD FILED A PROTEST OF THE OPENER OVER A LINEUP CARD SNAFU.

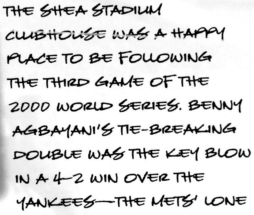

THE SHEA STADIUM CLUBHOUSE WAS A HAPPY PLACE TO BE FOLLOWING THE THIRD GAME OF THE 2000 WORLD SERIES. BENNY AGBAYANI'S TIE-BREAKING DOUBLE WAS THE KEY BLOW IN A 4-2 WIN OVER THE YANKEES—THE METS' LONE FALL CLASSIC VICTORY SINCE 1986.

ALTHOUGH THE ONLY METS UNIFORM NUMBERS TO HAVE BEEN OFFICIALLY RETIRED ARE #37 (CASEY STENGEL), #14 (GIL HODGES), AND #41 (TOM SEAVER), THEY HAVE NOT ISSUED MIKE PIAZZA'S #31 TO ANOTHER PLAYER SINCE THE HEAVY-HITTING CATCHER DEPARTED IN 2005.

CHAPTER SIX

AS NEW YORK REBUILDS, SO DO THE METS

2001–2009

THE SINE WAVE that has been the narration of the Mets franchise took another plunge after the exhilarating 2000 season. With their city under the specter of terror-ism after September 11, 2001, the Mets temporarily became "America's team," but ultimately not even a bloated payroll could break the fall. By mid-decade, new management on the field and off had plot-ted a fresh direction—one that led from a decrepit stadium to the fertile baseball landscape of Latin America and back to a glimmering new home.

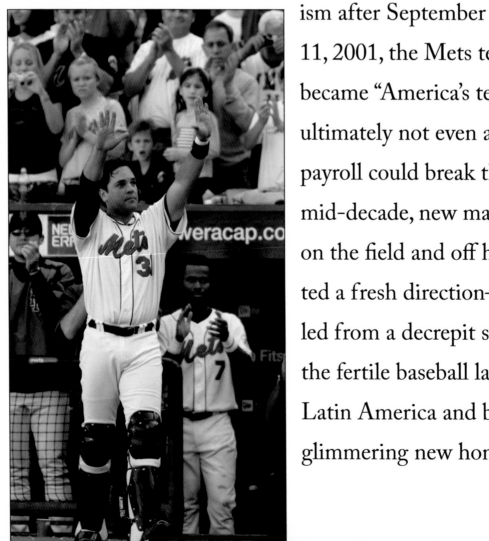

Knowing that he would not be re-signed, fans show-ered Mike Piazza with gratitude on October 2, 2005, in recogni-tion of his seven-plus seasons of thrills. The Hall of Fame-bound catcher represented the club on six All-Star teams, won four Silver Sluggers, and gave fans innumer-able "Mets moments."

This stadium give-away, which cel-ebrated the 2000 NL pennant, measured 8×6 inches. The real one now hangs at Citi Field along with those from 1969, 1973, and 1986. The Dodgers fly more (21) than any other NL franchise—nine of them since they left New York.

WATERHOUSE
NEW YORK
Mets
NATIONAL LEAGUE CHAMPIONS
2000

Feedback regarding the new home of the Mets was overwhelmingly positive. Keith Hernandez, one of the many franchise luminaries in attendance at its inauguration, said, "aesthetically, physically, I think it is the best ballpark I've seen."

In Piazza's Hands, a City Takes Heart

As the world watched New York City's response to the 9/11 attacks, Mike Piazza watched his game-winning home run in the first game at Shea following the tragedy. It may not have been the most consequential swing by a Met, but it was perhaps the most important.

The most significant things that ever happened at Shea Stadium did not involve Tom Seaver, Bill Buckner, The Beatles, or the Pope—they were, instead, the delivery of food and supply pallets to its gates, the rigging of makeshift lodging for scores of sleepless heroes, and the buoyant reopening of its doors for baseball after ten days of unspeakable distress.

The game between the Mets and Braves on September 21, 2001, was the first major sporting event in New York City following the terrorist attacks on the World Trade Center. The citizens of the violated city craved the semblance of normalcy that the game could provide. And Shea, after serving as a sanctuary for rescue workers the previous week, was ready to deliver.

The proceedings were less a competition than an exhalation of commemoration, mourning, prayer, and even celebration. Before the game, New York's finest—its firefighters, police, EMTs, and countless volunteers—were honored, and the two teams shook hands in solidarity. Diana Ross belted out "God Bless America" and Liza Minnelli's seventh-inning rendition of "New York, New York" melted the 41,235 sad and frazzled fans.

In the eighth inning, Mike Piazza guaranteed that the symbolism of the evening—that neither Gotham nor the great game of baseball entwined into its tradition could be cowed by the scourge and scars of fanaticism. Batting with a man aboard and his Mets trailing 2–1, the indomitable catcher delivered the biggest swing of his career on a stage that was more illuminated and important than any World Series. His home run bore more than victory for a team—it carried the very spirit of a city. Armando Benitez's save fulfilled the catharsis, and for this one brief interlude from anguish, all the Mets were saviors.

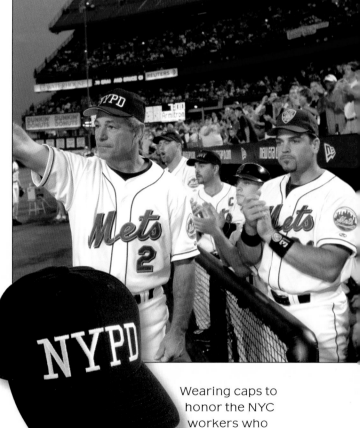

Wearing caps to honor the NYC workers who responded to the 9/11 crisis, Bobby Valentine and Mike Piazza saluted Mayor Rudy Giuliani as the team returned to Shea on September 21.

An Old Story…but a New Direction

Mirroring the disappointing aftermath of the 1986 world championship, expectations for a post-Subway Series Mets dynasty never materialized. The Steve Phillips–Bobby Valentine collaboration—much like that of Frank Cashen and Davey Johnson in the late '80s—fell apart with startling rapidity, both in cohesion and consequences.

The general manager broke his own rules of engagement—after 2000, Phillips seemed to neglect player makeup and team chemistry in favor of indulgent expenditures for dete-

Mo Vaughn, a former AL MVP with the Red Sox, was acquired in December 2001 to add power and presence. In 2002, he provided too little of one (posting a disappointing 72 RBI) and too much of the other (weighing in at a pudgy 275 pounds).

riorating and often indifferent former stars such as Mo Vaughn, Roberto Alomar, Jeromy Burnitz, and Kevin Appier. Concurrently, the farm system fell into disrepair. Meanwhile, the brassy skipper seemed to shed whatever thin filter had previously veiled his ego and, in the process, forfeited credibility with the front office and his players.

Before buying 50 percent of the Mets in 1986, owner Fred Wilpon purchased a 1 percent stake in the team in 1980.

Valentine was fired following the team's fifth-place finish of 2002, and Phillips did not survive '03. Art Howe, a Phillips appointee, (mis)managed the team on the field for two futile seasons while the young Jim Duquette seemed overmatched in his brief year-plus stint in the GM chair. The team's sole marketable stars, Mike Piazza and Al Leiter, were nearing the ends of their on-field usefulness. Most ominously, the team's bloated payroll—the largest in the National League—was generating its 11th-ranked attendance.

Fred Wilpon had seen enough. The emotionally invested CEO had navigated a legal battle with Nelson Doubleday Jr. to become the team's sole owner and decided to take the bull by the horns. The winter of 2004 was a time of transformation for the Mets. A refurbished management strategy required refurbished management. Wilpon found half of his dream team across the border and the other half right across town.

METS MEMORABILIA

A FORMER SHEA STADIUM VENDOR ONCE HIJACKED THE METS BULLPEN BUGGY AND TOOK IT FOR A SPIN IN THE OUTFIELD AFTER THE TEAM CLINCHED THE NL EAST IN 1986—THE FUN DIED WHEN THE CAR'S BATTERY DID.

IT WAS WITH A HEAVY HEART THAT JOHN FRANCO WORE A JERSEY WITH "9-11-01" INSCRIBED ON THE SLEEVE. THE NYC DEPARTMENT OF SANITATION, FOR WHICH THE RELIEF ACE'S FATHER FORMERLY WORKED, REMOVED OVER ONE MILLION TONS OF DEBRIS FROM THE SITE OF THE TERRORIST ATTACKS.

SATURDAY, SEPTEMBER 22, 2001 SPORTS ★ ★ ★ FINAL

STAR & STRIPES

Sports
AMERICA'S NO.1 SPORTS SECTION

Piazza, Mets sink Braves in emotional return home

Mike Piazza points skyward after eighth-inning homer rallies Mets past Braves, 3-2, on patriotic and dramatic night at Shea as baseball returns to city. Win pulls Mets within 4½ games of first-place Atlanta. Pages 62-64

RIVERA FOR THE BIRDS
Orioles rally in ninth to top Yanks — McCarron, Pages 65-66

MIKE PIAZZA WILL ALWAYS BE KNOWN AS A METS LEGEND AND HERO. THOSE QUALITIES WERE NEVER MORE APPARENT THAN WHEN HE BLASTED A HOME RUN TO WIN THE FIRST GAME PLAYED IN NEW YORK AFTER 9/11.

NEW YORK LOST TO CINCINNATI ON TOM GLAVINE "BOBBLEHEAD NIGHT" AT SHEA ON JULY 26, 2003, BUT THE HUMAN VERSION OF THE PITCHER IS ONE OF ONLY SIX LEFT-HANDERS TO WIN 300 GAMES. SIXTY-ONE OF THOSE WINS CAME IN FIVE SEASONS WITH THE METS.

THIS STATUE IS EIGHT INCHES TALL, BUT ONE THAT STOOD EIGHT FEET TALL WAS PLACED AT PENN STATION IN NEW YORK AS PART OF MAJOR LEAGUE BASEBALL'S PROMOTION OF THE 2008 ALL-STAR GAME AT YANKEE STADIUM.

FOR 16 YEARS IN ATLANTA, TOM GLAVINE WAS A METS NEMESIS, DEFEATING THEM 16 TIMES IN 23 DECISIONS. HE SIGNED WITH NEW YORK IN 2003, AND HE WORE THIS JERSEY AS A 40-YEAR-OLD ALL-STAR IN '06. TWO YEARS LATER, HE RETURNED TO THE BRAVES—AND BEAT THE METS FOR ONE OF HIS TWO WINS THAT YEAR.

The Latin Connection

Fred Wilpon had his eye on Montreal GM Omar Minaya for a long time, and at the conclusion of the 2004 season, the owner blinked. He lured Minaya away from the Expos, offering total control and a big budget to resuscitate the moribund Mets. "I just want Omar to be Omar," was Wilpon's sales pitch.

The Dominican-born executive, who spent most of his childhood in Queens, was baseball's first Hispanic GM. As such, he arrived with no weightier credential than an ability to capitalize on his heritage to attract Latin stars.

Within months, the best hitter (Carlos Beltran) and the best pitcher (Pedro Martinez) on the free-agent market had become Mets. It was a symbiotic celebration—the former's first seven home runs in a Mets uniform came in the latter's starts. In a *Daily News* poll asking who was "The Man" in New York sports, the effervescent Martinez outpolled Yankee icons Derek Jeter and Alex Rodriguez.

The pilgrimage continued. In 2006, the Mets' roster contained nearly twice as many Latinos as other teams, on average. So pervasive were the tropical leanings that they came to be called *Los Mets*—a term Minaya considers quasi-racist.

"I knew there'd be criticism about the ethnic makeup of the team," he told *Sports Illustrated*. "When you're the first Latino GM, you know it's coming. But I don't care about players' color, religion, heritage or even sexual preference. I care about winning today. I'll go to sleep tonight thinking, How can we make this team better?"

Minaya's inclusiveness made the team better in a hurry. The improvement was expedited with the hiring of former Yankee coach Willie Randolph (who grew up in Brooklyn and had a lifetime of local experience) as the club's first African American manager prior to the 2005 campaign. In Randolph's first season, the Mets snapped their three-year losing skid, and in 2006, they were back in the playoffs. It was just Omar being Omar.

Despite some ineffectual personnel moves and a few uncharacteristic PR lapses, GM Omar Minaya is admired as a self-made baseball man who pulled himself out of poverty in Queens; he started as a minor-league short-timer before rising to scout, then ultimately, to front-office *wunderkind*.

Growin' Your Own

The fruits of the Mets' farm system have not often been left to ripen on the vine; instead, they have been shipped out for more (presumably) accomplished veterans. Since 2005, however, the left side of the diamond has been staffed by the two most talented infielders the organization has ever developed—and had the good sense to retain.

Third baseman David Wright is the blue-and-orange rejoinder to pin-striped deity Derek Jeter across town—the face of the Mets franchise because of his brilliant play and refreshing decency in an era of discredited icons. "David," said GM Omar Minaya, "is someone you build around not only as a player but also as a person."

From the 2004 winter day on which they refused to send Wright to Seattle for the rights to hire away manager Lou Piniella, the Mets have done just that.

Wright's subsequent summers have yielded two Gold Gloves, two Silver Sluggers, and four of the nine .300-AVG/30-HR/100-RBI/15-SB seasons in major-league history by a third baseman. And he's done it with class and accessibility. "When I put my head on my pillow after my career's over," said Wright, the son of a Virginia police officer, "I want to tell myself I became the best player I possibly could doing things the right way."

To Wright's left stands Jose Reyes, a supercharged switch-hitter who led the league in stolen bases and triples three times apiece before his 26th birthday. The two-time All-Star, who was signed out of a Dominican try-out camp as a scrawny teen in 1999, inflames the offense from the leadoff spot and solidifies the defense with his flamboyant shortstop play.

Since the pair reached New York to stay in 2004, nearly 200 different players have sprouted on the Mets rosters. A great deal of lettuce has been tossed at pricey acquisitions, but Wright and Reyes have proven that, in the field of dreams, there's nothing quite like homegrown.

New Yorkers appreciate not only Wright's ability, but his background as the son of a police officer and his unaffected, dirty-uni style of play. In 2006, Delta Air Lines named its NYC–Boston–DC shuttle after him—"The Wright Flight."

Above: Said Pedro Martinez of Jose Reyes—perhaps the most athletic player in Mets history—"When I'm finished, I'll get the best seat to see him play. I'll pay whatever price to see him."

Left: Jose Reyes was invited to the All-Star Game two summers in a row. He sat out the first with an injury, but made the Mets proud by rapping a double and two singles, scoring a run, and stealing a base in 2007.

A Return to October

In the 20th anniversary season of the Mets' 1986 world championship, history seemed ordained to repeat itself. The 2006 squad waltzed through its division and became the first team to dethrone Atlanta since the leagues were realigned in 1994. New York hogged first place from April 6 on and stretched its advantage to 16 and a half games by mid-September. The team's lights-out bullpen (led by Billy Wagner's 40 saves) and powerful offense covered for a precarious rotation. Carlos Beltran tied the team record with 41 home runs, Carlos Delgado added 38, and David Wright posted 26; all three sluggers notched at least 114 RBI. At the top of the lineup, Jose Reyes's speed-saturated smorgasbord of 64 steals, 30 doubles, 17 triples, and 19 homers added a dynamic dimension to the club's attack.

The Dodgers offered little resistance in the first round of the playoffs, falling in three straight. But then came the NLCS, and suddenly New York's 1986-style mojo turned to 1988-fashioned frustration.

At 83–78, the Cardinals had barely made the postseason and were expected by many to be summarily dismissed by New York. The Mets set about doing just that with a 2–0 Game 1 win, led by a seven-inning, four-hit effort by Tom Glavine (behind whom the team won 24 of 32 regular-season

starts). Seven pitchers failed to stave off a 9–6 ninth-inning loss in Game 2, however, and the bats were blanked the next night, 5–0. The Mets bounced back as Beltran, Delgado, and Wright combined for four homers in a 12–5 Game 4 rout. The teams exchanged 4–2 victories in Games 5 and 6 to set up a decisive Game 7.

Cobbling together a rotation gashed by the loss of sore-shouldered Pedro Martinez, Willie Randolph was forced to send Oliver Perez—a wild young lefty who posted three

The 97–65 Mets coulda-shoulda-woulda had something more to celebrate than just a divisional title in 2006, but at least that was something to hang their Santa hat on when they mailed out this official corporate Christmas card the following winter.

Endy Chavez's catch of a Scott Rolen drive saved Game 7 of the 2006 NLCS, but only temporarily. "I jumped as high as I can—like a 10 percent chance in my mind I could catch it," he said. "See the ball, see the wall, and do the thing that I've got to do."

regular-season wins and a 6.55 ERA—to the hill in a sudden-death scenario. Perez came up big, giving up just one run in six innings. The 1–1 tie was preserved in the sixth inning by one of the greatest plays in postseason history—Endy Chavez leapt up and over the left-field wall to thieve a two-run homer from Scott Rolen, then fired the ball back into the infield to double up Jim Edmonds.

The deadlock persisted into the ninth, when déjà vu grabbed a Cardinals bat. Yadier Molina—like the Dodgers' Mike Scioscia, who had delivered the crippling home run of the 1988 NLCS—was a weak-hitting catcher.

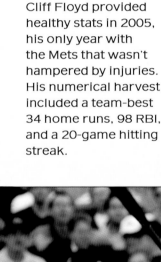

Cliff Floyd provided healthy stats in 2005, his only year with the Mets that wasn't hampered by injuries. His numerical harvest included a team-best 34 home runs, 98 RBI, and a 20-game hitting streak.

Slam! Slam!

On July 16, for 41 minutes on a 95-degree night at Chicago's Wrigley Field, the Mets were *en fuego.* When the smoke cleared, they had combusted for a team-record 11-run sixth inning.

Two of the 70 pitches in the frame were turned around for grand slams (by Cliff Floyd and Carlos Beltran), and a third's fate was a two-run homer by David Wright. Sixteen Mets came to the plate, with Wright and Carlos Delgado contributing two hits apiece. At one point, action was paused while the grounds crew cleared debris that had been chucked onto the field by disgusted Chicago fans. The final damage: Mets 13, Cubs 7.

Cliff Floyd's slam on this swing was just the opening salvo of the team's biggest inning ever. He was one of five Mets to reach base twice.

But on this day, he was a hero—his two-run roundtripper shot St. Louis ahead, 3–1. The Mets attempted to invoke the ghost of Bill Buckner after loading the bases in the bottom of the inning, but no such apparition would manifest. Beltran froze at a called third strike, leaving Mets fans to commiserate on the collapse of what was, most agreed, the best team in baseball. The "C word"—choke—was just commencing its lengthy haunt of their lexicon.

Oliver Perez's finest moment as a Met kept his team in Game 7 of the 2006 NLCS. He won 15 games the next season, but he has been one of the wildest pitchers in baseball since then.

METS MEMORABILIA

A TRADE FOR JOHAN SANTANA JUST BEFORE SPRING TRAINING IN 2008 RECAST THE METS AS FAVORITES TO GO ALL THE WAY. THEY DIDN'T QUITE GET IT DONE, BUT THEIR NEW ACE BEAT THE MARLINS ON OPENING DAY AND WENT ON TO LEAD THE NL IN ERA.

WILLIE RANDOLPH'S HIGHLIGHTED SCORECARD FROM GAME 2 OF THE 2006 NLCS WAS ETCHED WITH LOWLIGHTS. CARLOS DELGADO HOMERED TWICE, BUT CLOSER BILLY WAGNER LET A TIE GAME GET AWAY IN THE NINTH AS THE CARDS WON, 9-6, TO EVEN THE SERIES.

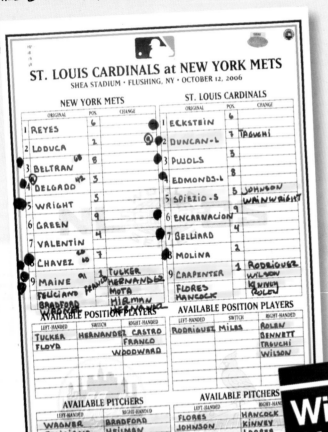

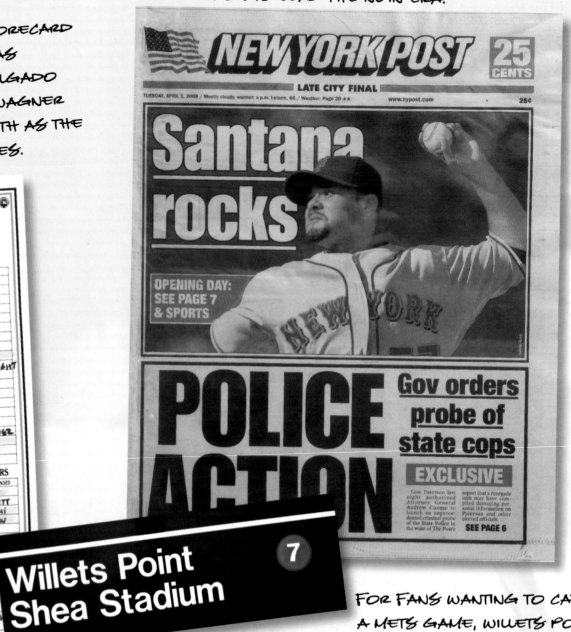

FOR FANS WANTING TO CATCH A METS GAME, WILLETS POINT IS THE SUBWAY STOP AT ROOSEVELT & 126TH. A LONG-BLIGHTED NEIGHBORHOOD, THE SITE OF THE FILM *CHOP SHOP* IS CURRENTLY UNDERGOING REDEVELOPMENT.

DAVID WRIGHT IS THE 25TH DIFFERENT MET TO WEAR #5. THE FIRST WAS LITERALLY THE FIRST—HOBIE LANDRITH WAS THE INITIAL PLAYER THE CLUB CHOSE IN THE EXPANSION DRAFT THAT STOCKED ITS FIRST ROSTER.

THIS CARLOS DELGADO BOBBLEHEAD WAS SPONSORED IN 2007 BY P. C. RICHARD & SON, AN ELECTRONICS MERCHANT THAT STARTED WITH A HARDWARE STORE IN BROOKLYN IN 1909. ITS MOTTO, "HONESTY, INTEGRITY AND RELIABILITY," COULD EASILY APPLY TO THE METS' CLASSY FIRST BASEMAN.

THIS BASE WAS IN PLAY FOR THE FIRST THREE INNINGS OF A GAME WITH THE YANKEES AT SHEA ON MAY 19, 2006, THEN SAFELY AUTHENTICATED FOR SALE BY THE TIME DAVID WRIGHT SINGLED OFF (USUALLY) UNTOUCHABLE CLOSER MARIANO RIVERA FOR THE GAME-WINNER IN THE NINTH.

DURING SHEA'S SWAN SONG SEASON, THE METS SCHEDULED 35 PROMOTIONAL DATES DURING WHICH THEY DISBURSED MORE THAN A HALF-MILLION UNITS OF SWAG—EVERYTHING FROM BEARS TO BOBBLEHEADS TO BAGS TO BLANKETS, AND THIS OLD-SCHOOL LUNCH BOX.

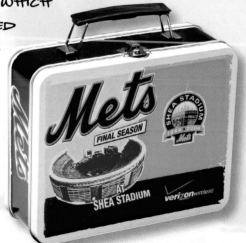

Dollar-Wi$e or Non-Cent$?

Second baseman Kazuo Matsui failed to meet expectations after arriving from Japan, but he claimed an oddball nook in the major-league record book as the first player ever to hit a home run in the first at-bat of each of his first three seasons.

When Omar Minaya was hired, Fred Wilpon essentially presented him with a book of blank checks, and the owner has been more than happy to autograph them ever since. Not since the parsimonious pair of Charles Payson and M. Donald Grant locked the safe in the late 1970s has money ever been an object for the Mets, whose payroll has been among baseball's six highest for over a decade.

A fading Mike Piazza was still due $16 million and the 39-year-old Tom Glavine was in the middle of a $42.5 million deal when Minaya came aboard, but he swiftly committed $119 million for seven years of center fielder Carlos Beltran's services and $53 million for four years of Pedro Martinez. He tried very hard to give Carlos Delgado $50 million more, but the first baseman signed with the Marlins, only to join the Mets in a trade after one season in Florida.

In 2004, it cost the club $20 million to import second baseman Kaz Matsui from Japan; two years later, $43 million was doled out to address a dire need for a closer by inking Billy Wagner for four years. Senior citizens Moises Alou (40 years old), Shawn Green (34), and Orlando Hernandez (41 . . . allegedly) were added to the 2007–08 books for a total of $36.5 million. Heading into 2008, Minaya gave Johan Santana the richest contract for a pitcher in the history of the game at the time—$137.5 million for six years. Still desperate for pitching in '09, he signed Francisco Rodriguez for three years and $37 million and showered the infuriatingly shaky Oliver Perez with $36 million over three years.

None of those zillionaires have avoided sharp performance decline, major injury or both, and the farm system hasn't produced an above-average Met since David Wright came up in 2004. The opening of Citi Field in 2009 allowed Wilpon to print a little more cash, but the flagging bang-for-buck ratio and overall economic climate slowed the presses.

Postseason failures and elbow surgery that cost him a year's worth of action besmirched an otherwise commendable stint for Billy Wagner as the Mets' closer— 101 saves and a 2.40 ERA from 2006 to '08. He returned briefly to the team in '09 before being dealt to the Boston Red Sox.

Carlos & Carlos

This game-ending home run trot in August was the second of the 2006 season for the ever-clutch Carlos Beltran. In July, he hit a homer in three consecutive plate appearances with the bases loaded.

Some teams dip their toes in the personnel pools; others take an occasional swim. That cannonball splash? That's usually the Mets.

There was no higher-profile player in the trade or free-agent markets after the 2004 season than Carlos Beltran, whose near-40–40 season vaulted him to the top of Omar Minaya's Christmas list. Soon after the holidays, at the cost of the tenth $100-million-plus contract in baseball history, he got his man.

For a year, the center fielder looked like coal in the GM's stocking. But when Willie Randolph was able to stack Beltran back-to-back in the order with Puerto Rican countryman Carlos Delgado in '06, both veteran stars flourished.

Delgado struck a commanding presence. The first baseman brought a string of nine straight 30-homer seasons to New York, and then hit 100 more over his first three campaigns for the Mets. A smart and thoughtful man who grew up idolizing Roberto Clemente, he poured his heart into humanitarian causes and social activism—although he's become more private since inciting a tempest while with the Blue Jays by refusing to leave the dugout for "God Bless America" as a political protest. Between the lines, his loudest day in a Mets uniform came on June 27, 2008, when his team-record nine RBI powered a demolition of the Yankees.

Beltran proved a parallel force. From '06 to '08, he out-homered Delgado by one, topped 100 RBI each season, built upon his all-time big-league record for stolen base percentage and earned the only three Gold Gloves by a Mets outfielder since Tommie Agee.

The 2009 campaign saw both players fall to major injuries. Though Beltran had two years remaining on his pact following the season, the 37-year-old Delgado became a free agent. The Carlos & Carlos show may have moved off-Broadway without a championship, but it was worth the price of admission.

Prior to his hip injury in 2009, Carlos Delgado gave the Mets three seasons of distinction on the field and dignity off it. The all-time home run and RBI leader among Puerto Rico-born players averaged 33 and 105, respectively, from '06 to '08.

Twice to the Brink, Twice Denied

Following the games of September 12, 2007, the dataheads at BaseballProspectus.com played out the remainder of the season through one million computer simulations. In more than 998,000 of them, the Mets made the playoffs.

This outcome seemed reasonable, since New York led Philadelphia by seven games in the NL East standings and no team with a lead of at least seven games on that date had ever failed to advance to the postseason. Predictability, however, has never been a hallmark of the Mets franchise. Losses—including a humiliating sweep at Shea at the hands of the woeful Nationals—mounted while the Phillies played red-hot baseball. On on the 28th, with two games remaining, New York's 135-day stranglehold on the NL East lead ended. And on the season's final day, so did its playoff aspirations, positioning everything from the team's character to Willie Randolph's job in the crosshairs.

Minaya, though, kept his hatchet holstered over the winter and boldly traded for Johan Santana—the consensus best pitcher in baseball. But a 2008 season that had been projected as redemption crumbled into replay.

Although David Wright's bat was "punished" after a called third strike in this 2007 contest, it didn't do much else wrong that season. The young third baseman won his first of back-to-back Silver Slugger Awards by hitting .325 with 30 homers.

The Fall Guy

In New York, leashes come in only one size: extra-short. And when Willie Randolph reached the end of his in 2008, he was treated like a dog.

Although Randolph was considered a pro's pro and had won a higher percentage of games than any other Met field boss save Davey Johnson, Omar Minaya felt his team was too talented to be sitting a game under .500 in June. He had effectively withdrawn his support for Randolph long before, turning the media into piranha and his manager into a pariah. Still, Minaya allowed his scapegoat to fly to the West Coast and win a game before announcing his dismissal in an e-mail that was sent at 3 A.M.

"I love Willie Randolph," Minaya rationalized, "but this wasn't about love." Nor was it about patience, timing or—some would say—class.

Willie Randolph has six World Series rings, each earned in New York, but none as a Met. The former Yankees player and coach brought wins and class to the Mets, but led the team to just one divisional title.

Randolph was fired after 69 games, and although successor Jerry Manuel managed to guide the team back to the top of the NL East for a month, the Mets lost nine of their last 16 and ceded first to Philadelphia on September 20. With a defeat to the Marlins in the final game ever at Shea Stadium, even their chance at a Wild Card vanished.

"We failed," mourned David Wright. "Tough to swallow," lamented Jose Reyes. "I have no more words," whispered Carlos Beltran. Even the words, "Wait 'til next year" rang hollow.

Citi Field

The closing of antiquated Shea Stadium in 2008 was bittersweet for Mets fans. The disillusionment of recent seasons was as stubborn to eradicate as the astringent odor permanently absorbed into its restrooms. On the other hand, the blissful memories were just as thick—of Casey quotes, a say "hey" to Willie, the miracle of '69, Tom's terrific-ness, the unbelievable pennant of '88, Doc's house calls (and so many Mets close calls), Darryl's dingers, Piazza's pokes, and most of all, those gut-wrenching Game 6s.

On April 13, 2009, the newly built Citi Field began marshaling its own nostalgia. Fans parked on the ashes of Shea and beheld a gorgeous brick façade reminiscent of Ebbets Field. They entered through the Jackie Robinson Rotunda and proceeded through warm, bustling concourses to a hub of 42,000 seats—15,000 fewer than its predecessor. The field itself revealed an intriguing configuration of seven distinct dimensions along the outfield wall. Beyond it in straightaway center lurked the "Big Apple"—a refurbished version of the old Shea trademark that popped up after every Mets round-tripper since 1980. (When the club surveyed fans about which vestige of Shea they most wanted retained, 89 percent insisted on the Apple.)

Five-star reviews poured in for the Mets' new digs. Pundits particularly hailed its classy simplicity—especially as compared to the ostentatious reincarnation of Yankee Stadium (called "The House That Greed Built" by Phil Mushnick of the *New York Post*) that would be unveiled three days later at twice the price tag.

Even the environmentally friendly, waterless restrooms were beyond reproach. Well, almost—in May, a patron was found shrieking for help after getting her arm stuck in a toilet while trying to retrieve her gold tooth. Citi Field—like the Mets themselves—is proving to be, if not always perfect, at least always interesting.

This novelty timepiece is a replica of the famous "Home Run Apple" that rose out of a hat beyond the Shea Stadium fence whenever a Met clocked a home run. A larger version of the animatronic attraction was installed at Citi Field in 2009.

METS MEMORABILIA

IN 2009, NASA ASTRONAUT AND ZEALOUS METS FAN MIKE MASSIMINO TOOK SHEA STADIUM'S HOME PLATE WITH HIM ON A 5.2-MILLION-MILE TRIP TO REPAIR THE HUBBLE SPACE TELESCOPE. BACK ON EARTH, THE DISH IS NOW DISPLAYED AT CITI FIELD.

THE METS ISSUED THIS COMMEMORATIVE BALL WHEN THEY CHRISTENED CITI FIELD WITH TWO CHARITY EXHIBITION GAMES AGAINST THE RED SOX. NEW YORK TOOK THE FIRST GAME, 4-3, BUT LOST THE SECOND, 9-3.

JOHAN SANTANA, THE BRILLIANT LEFT-HANDER, IS BY FAR THE MOST NOTABLE WEARER OF JERSEY #57 FOR THE METS. ITS OTHER INHABITANTS HAVE BEEN COACHES BOBBY FLOYD AND TOM ROBSON, PITCHER JASON ROACH, AND OUTFIELDER ERIC VALENT.

WILLIE RANDOLPH WAS A LOCAL PRODUCT, A SOUND MANAGER AND A GOOD MAN, BUT BY THE TIME HE HAD HIS BOBBLEHEAD DAY AT SHEA IN 2007, HIS STAR HAD DIMMED—PRIMARILY BECAUSE OF THE TEAM'S STUNNING '06 NLCS DEFEAT. HE WAS DISMISSED MIDWAY THROUGH '08, WHEN HIS TEAM BOBBLED OUT OF THE GATE 34-35.

WILLIE RANDOLPH

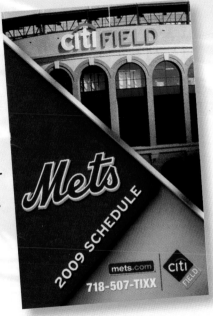

MEMENTOS OF THE FIRST SEASON OF PLAY AT CITI FIELD ABOUND, INCLUDING THE TEAM'S OFFICIAL POCKET SCHEDULE.

A 48-PAGE SPECIAL SECTION OF THE DAILY NEWS SERVED AS HOMAGE TO CITI FIELD ON THE DAY BEFORE THE 2009 SEASON OPENED. THE NEWSPAPER CALLED IT A "180-DEGREE DEPARTURE FROM SHEA STADIUM"— AND MEANT THAT IN A GOOD WAY.

A Season Cursed, but Hope Renewed

It was September 9, and the Mets took their positions for the official 2009 team photo. There they were—Carlos Beltran, Jose Reyes, Johan Santana, Carlos Delgado, David Wright, John Maine, Gary Sheffield—all of them together in uniform for the first time since, oh when? Opening Day?

Pretty much.

The season had begun with vows to rinse the acid tang of two successive late-season meltdowns. The sheen of Citi Field beckoned a stacked $136-million roster whose one previous flaw—a bullpen disemboweled by Billy Wagner's September elbow surgery—had been audaciously addressed with the signing of record-setting closer Francisco Rodriguez and the acquisition of another relief arm, J. J. Putz, from Seattle in a massive three-team, 11-player deal. On May 29, the Mets were perched atop the NL East following a dramatic win over the Marlins. It would be their last view from the top.

At that point, nine players already populated the disabled list. Two of them—Delgado (hip) and Reyes (hamstring)—were indispensable stars who would not return to action all season. The carnage never abated. In June, Beltran injured his knee and starter Maine his shoulder; both would miss ten weeks. DL assignments reached 20 by August when Wright took a pitch to his dome and Santana submitted to elbow surgery. The pitcher's demise was the team's deathblow: The defending NL ERA champ was on his way to

another stunner of a season when the pain became too much.

By July 21, the Mets were ten games out of first, a deficit that would double two months later. The attrition took its toll even on the ambulatory, as the team often seemed stupefied, squandering games on base-running blunders and flubs of routine plays (most memorably a dropped pop-up by second baseman Luis Castillo that cost the team its June 12 game against the Yankees). But with a major league-high 1,480 games lost to the DL by eight former All-Stars whose career home run total exceeded 1,000, the club was beyond redemption, finishing with a 70–92 record.

The adversity was hardly a measure of manager Jerry Manuel, who was obliged to deploy more than 50 different players. In his first full season, Willie Randolph's successor stayed positive and largely above Gotham's fishbowl scrutiny. Most of that was focused on Omar

There could be no other choice than Tom Seaver to toss out the first pitch prior to the Mets' opening game at Citi Field. "It's almost like yesterday, the emotion that I had," the 64-year-old immortal reflected afterward. The Mets can only hope for similarly Terrific tomorrows.

140

Minaya, who was skewered in the media for bungling allegations of misconduct by a team VP, then for unleashing a bizarre harangue on a reporter.

So as Citi Field closed its doors on its melancholic maiden campaign, the euphoria of opening day seemed far removed. But it was not a circumstance with which the franchise and its partisans were unfamiliar, nor unequipped to address.

It was into adversity that the team had been born, and it was out of it that its greatest successes had been realized. When New York was deserted by the Giants and Dodgers,

the Mets filled the chasm. Fans, in turn, abided the follies of the early years and were soon rewarded with a miracle. They believed against all odds in 1973 and were vindicated. Their heroes were down to their final swing in '86, but prevailed. When the city's very way of life was under assault after September 11, the faithful migrated to the ballpark for relief, and their pain was eased. The sacred symbiosis has entered its third generation, and neither two September swoons nor one cursed season can violate it. In an organization rich with talent and resources, buoyed by a steadfast Mets Nation, renewal has already begun.

Citi Field opened to great fanfare and ceremony on April 13, 2009. As the cast of the Broadway revival of *West Side Story* performed the National Anthem, a quartet of U.S. Marine F-18 Hornets executed a dramatic flyover.

LEADERS AND LEGENDS

Team History

World Series Winners
1969, 1986

Pennant Winners
1969, 1973, 1986, 2000

Division Winners
1969, 1973, 1986, 1988, 2006

Wild Card Winners
1999, 2000

Hall of Fame Members
Richie Ashburn, CF (1962)
Yogi Berra, C (1965); Mgr. (1972–75)
Gary Carter, C (1985–89)
Rickey Henderson, LF (1999–2000)
Willie Mays, CF (1972–73)
Eddie Murray, 1B (1992–93)
Nolan Ryan, P (1966, 1968–71)
Tom Seaver, P (1967–77, 1983)*
Duke Snider, CF (1963)
Warren Spahn, P (1965)
Casey Stengel, Mgr. (1962–65)
Mets logo on plaque

Retired Uniform Numbers
Gil Hodges—14
Casey Stengel—37
Tom Seaver—41
Jackie Robinson—42#
 # retired by all major-league clubs

Award Winners

NL Cy Young Award
1969—Tom Seaver
1973—Tom Seaver
1975—Tom Seaver
1985—Dwight Gooden

NL Rookie of the Year
1967—Tom Seaver, P
1972—Jon Matlack, P
1983—Darryl Strawberry, OF
1984—Dwight Gooden, P

NL Gold Glove
1970—Tommie Agee, OF
1971—Bud Harrelson, SS
1980—Doug Flynn, 2B
1983—Keith Hernandez, 1B
1984—Keith Hernandez, 1B
1985—Keith Hernandez, 1B
1986—Keith Hernandez, 1B
1987—Keith Hernandez, 1B
1988—Keith Hernandez, 1B
1989—Ron Darling, P
1997—Rey Ordonez, SS
1998—Rey Ordonez, SS
1999—Rey Ordonez, SS
1999—Robin Ventura, 3B
2006—Carlos Beltran, OF
2007—Carlos Beltran, OF
2007—David Wright, 3B
2008—Carlos Beltran, OF
2008—David Wright, 3B

NL Silver Slugger
1984—Keith Hernandez, 1B
1985—Gary Carter, C
1986—Gary Carter, C
1988—Darryl Strawberry, OF
1989—Howard Johnson, 3B
1990—Darryl Strawberry, OF
1991—Howard Johnson, 3B
1992—Dwight Gooden, P
1998—Mike Piazza, C
1999—Mike Piazza, C
1999—Edgardo Alfonzo, 2B
2000—Mike Piazza, C
2000—Mike Hampton, P
2001—Mike Piazza, C
2002—Mike Piazza, C
2006—Jose Reyes, SS
2006—Carlos Beltran, OF
2007—Carlos Beltran, OF
2007—David Wright, 3B
2008—David Wright, 3B

NL Rolaids Relief Man
1990—John Franco
2001—Armando Benitez

World Series MVP
1969—Donn Clendenon
1969—Al Weis (BBWAA)
1986—Ray Knight (BBWAA)

NLCS MVP
2000—Mike Hampton, P

Executive of the Year
1969—Johnny Murphy
1986—Frank Cashen

Batting Leaders

League Leaders

Home Runs
1982—Dave Kingman, 37
1988—Darryl Strawberry, 39
1991—Howard Johnson, 38

Runs Batted In
1991—Howard Johnson, 117

Stolen Bases
2005—Jose Reyes, 60
2006—Jose Reyes, 64
2007—Jose Reyes, 78

Team Leaders

Average
John Olerud—.315
David Wright—.309
Keith Hernandez—.297
Mike Piazza—.296
Dave Magadan—.292
Edgardo Alfonzo—.292
Steve Henderson—.287
Jose Reyes—.286
Wally Backman—.283
Ron Hunt—.282

Home Runs
Darryl Strawberry—252
Mike Piazza—220
Howard Johnson—192
Dave Kingman—154
David Wright—140
Carlos Beltran—127
Todd Hundley—124
Kevin McReynolds—122
Edgardo Alfonzo—120
Ed Kranepool—118

It was Eddie Kranepool's signature that occupied the spot of honor on this bat signed by members of the 1973 NL-champion Mets. Krane didn't have a great year (only one home run), but with 12 continuous years of service, he was the squad's "greybeard" at age 28.

Runs Batted In

Darryl Strawberry—733
Mike Piazza—655
Howard Johnson—629
Ed Kranepool—614
David Wright—561
Edgardo Alfonzo—538
Cleon Jones—521
Keith Hernandez—468
Carlos Beltran—466
Kevin McReynolds—456

Stolen Bases

Jose Reyes—301
Mookie Wilson—281
Howard Johnson—202
Darryl Strawberry—191
Lee Mazzilli—152
David Wright—119
Lenny Dykstra—116
Bud Harrelson—115
Wally Backman—106
Roger Cedeno—105

30-HR/30-SB Seasons

1987—Howard Johnson, 36/32
1987—Darryl Strawberry, 39/36
1989—Howard Johnson, 36/41
1991—Howard Johnson, 38/30
2007—David Wright, 30/34

Ford C. Frick was the commissioner of baseball at the time of the Mets' creation.

Pitching Leaders

League Leaders

Victories

1969—Tom Seaver, 25
1975—Tom Seaver, 22
1985—Dwight Gooden, 24

Earned Run Average

1970—Tom Seaver, 2.82
1971—Tom Seaver, 1.76
1973—Tom Seaver, 2.08
1978—Craig Swan, 2.43
1985—Dwight Gooden, 1.53
2008—Johan Santana, 2.53

Strikeouts

1970—Tom Seaver, 283
1971—Tom Seaver, 289
1973—Tom Seaver, 251
1975—Tom Seaver, 243
1976—Tom Seaver, 235
1984—Dwight Gooden, 276
1985—Dwight Gooden, 268
1990—David Cone, 233
1991—David Cone, 241

Saves

1990—John Franco, 33
1994—John Franco, 30

Team Leaders

Victories

Tom Seaver—198
Dwight Gooden—157
Jerry Koosman—140
Ron Darling—99
Sid Fernandez—98
Al Leiter—95
Jon Matlack—82
David Cone—81
Bobby Jones—74
Steve Trachsel—66

Though his Mets hat is presented here, the first professional cap donned by Casey Stengel was for the Kansas City Blues.

Earned Run Average

Tom Seaver—2.57
Jesse Orosco—2.73
Jon Matlack—3.03
Jerry Koosman—3.09
Dwight Gooden—3.099
John Franco—3.10
Bobby Ojeda—3.12
David Cone—3.13
Sid Fernandez—3.14

Strikeouts

Tom Seaver—2,541
Dwight Gooden—1,875
Jerry Koosman—1,799
Sid Fernandez—1,449
David Cone—1,172
Ron Darling—1,148
Al Leiter—1,106
Jon Matlack—1,023
Bobby Jones—714
Craig Swan—671

Shutouts

Tom Seaver—44
Jerry Koosman—26
Jon Matlack—26
Dwight Gooden—23
David Cone—15
Ron Darling—10
Al Jackson—10
Sid Fernandez—9
Bobby Ojeda—9
Gary Gentry—8

Saves

John Franco—276
Armando Benitez—160
Jesse Orosco—107
Billy Wagner—101
Tug McGraw—86
Roger McDowell—84
Neil Allen—69
Skip Lockwood—65
Braden Looper—57
Randy Myers—56

New York Mets All-Time Team

CATCHER: Mike Piazza
FIRST BASE: Keith Hernandez
SECOND BASE: Edgardo Alfonzo
THIRD BASE: David Wright
SHORTSTOP: Jose Reyes
RIGHT FIELD: Darryl Strawberry
CENTER FIELD: Mookie Wilson
LEFT FIELD: Cleon Jones
STARTING PITCHER: Tom Seaver
RELIEF PITCHER: John Franco
MANAGER: Gil Hodges

Gil Hodges wasn't the only "famous number 14" for the Mets—Ron Swoboda shared the uniform tag.

Index